Contents

SO-AIE-503

foreword

Lanny Smith, President, YLI Corporation

In this book you will meet, and get to know one of the most creative people I have ever had the pleasure of knowing. Laura Heine is a quilter, but first and foremost, she is an artist. During a 30-year career in advertising I have met, and worked with, some of the most respected and awarded art directors and illustrators in the world. I place Laura in that select company.

Laura's talent goes beyond technique and style. She isn't afraid to look at things differently than convention might suggest. In fact, she takes pleasure in "pushing the envelope," in not just breaking the rules, but redefining them.

Bottled

I first met Laura in Houston, Texas, in 1995. I was new with YLI and Laura was attending one of her first International Quilt Markets. In fact, she was one of the prizewinners. I was impressed. I knew very little about quilting and Laura knew little about YLI. In fact, I don't believe she had ever heard of our products or us. We did, however, share a common goal. She was interested in thread and I was interested in having her use our thread in her next quilt. I gave her several types of thread that day in exchange for the promise that she would use them and let us use the finished quilt in our next show.

Months passed and I forgot about our little deal, until she called. The quilt was finished and she was sending it that day. It was with great anticipation that I opened the box, but nothing could prepare me for the quilt inside. It was unlike any quilt I had ever seen. She had used the thread, our thread, lots of thread.

There was Jeans Stitch, variegated Jeans Stitch, and our Fine Metallic, stipple quilted throughout. Yards and yards of thread were used, and the color, well I was blown away by her use of color! This quilt was more than special because it used our thread. It was a work of art.

Bottled was the title of that quilt. Laura and the quilt changed the face of quilting as we knew it. Until then, no one used variegated thread in quilting. Until that day, few people associated YLI with quilting. A movement, a style, began that day opening the door for the creative use of decorative threads in the art of machine quilting.

Bottled was purchased by YLI and it travels with us to trade shows throughout the world. This wonderful quilt and its creator helped establish Jeans Stitch as a major new quilting thread and set the stage for YLI's emergence as a major player in the quilting industry.

As you read and study this book you will be challenged to look into your soul for the part of you that makes you unique. You will learn to take chances, to try things never tried before ... to Unleash Your Imagination.

Color Fusion

Fiberworks by Laura Heine

FIRST U.S. edition
published in 2001

© 2001 Laura Heine

Publisher & Chief Editor:
    Linda Chang Teufel
Cover Design:
    Diana Juratovac
Page Layout & Design:
    mesh design+communication, inc.
Photography:
    Larry Friar, except where noted

Publisher's Cataloging in Publication Data
Heine, Laura
Color Fusion:
Fiberworks by Laura Heine
1. Quilting
2. Machine quilting
3. Patchwork
I. Title
ISBN# 0-9641201-5-1
Library of Congress Card Number: 2001086192

Printed in Thailand
10   9   8   7   6   5   4   3   2

Dragon Threads

410 Canyon Drive North
Columbus, Ohio 43214
www.dragonthreads.com

Photo by Tilton

Dedication

I dedicate this book to my mother, **Willow Jeane Lyman**, the most supportive person I have. Look at me sew now Mom!

Appreciation

I want to thank Linda Teufel for her persistence with me to do a book with her! Her help in the development of this publication from start to finish was real dedication. The opportunity to know her personally has been a wonderful experience!

Special thanks to:

My two children, Jenna and Brandon, who tolerate my obsession and share my successes!

Lanny Smith of YLI who truly believed in me. Our relationship together strengthened each of us individually.

Pat Smith with Kings Road Imports. Her willingness to take my drawings and paintings and turn them into fabric has been totally unbelievable. She has incorporated myself, YLI and Kings Road to work as a team, promoting each other along the way. It has truly been an interesting and inspirational journey.

My first quilt teacher, Cheryl Wittmayer. She taught me the basics of quiltmaking and the basics of friendship.

My grandmother, Marjorie Berg, who introduced me to the needle early on in my life. We embroidered pillowcases together, and I carry those hand stitches in my heart even today.

My Aunt Arlene McDonald, for her "quick" lessons in watercolor painting! Much of what I learned was through watching her over the years...well before I ever knew I would need to paint.

To my shop manager, Anita Clayton, who believes she doesn't "make a difference". She is very knowledgeable, friendly and a great manager; without her I could not have written this book. Anita, your support and commitment have made a huge difference to me.

To my Fiberworks staff who are the most loyal group of women anyone could ever have. Thank you Shirley, Wanda, Kay, Cheryl, Virginia, Linda and Janet.

To my dear friend Dione Roberts whose unbelievable talent in stained glass has crossed over into quilting, opening up a whole new world for the two of us.

To my editors who helped iron out the wrinkles: Louise Cynkus, Shirley DeMars, Rosie Blackford, Willow Lyman, Cathy Daum, Iris Lee, Sonja Tugend, Kim Koloski and Mary Ann Weber.

And finally, my mother Willow Jeane Lyman. She provides me with unconditional love and support. She taught me to sew clothes despite many objections during my early years. She taught me to be independent, not to be afraid of life and that mistakes are only learning experiences. She taught me to keep the faith and remember that things could always be worse.

Introduction **by Laura Heine**

My father died when I was four years old. He had leukemia in a time when it was incurable. His leaving had a huge impact on much of my life. He was 26 years old, and he left my mother with three young children. She has told me that during the few weeks before his death, when she would visit him in the hospital, that he did not want to hear about the children. He needed to forget about us, because it was so painful for him to be leaving us behind. I just cannot imagine it myself, having two young children now.

But what had the largest impact on me was that he left nothing behind. No letter, no tangible article that I could grasp onto, something left especially for me. At times I think that this is very selfish. How could he think of that "stuff" when he was dying? But, I have made a point in my life to leave something behind-to leave a trail that my children could follow. They will know me and remember what I did.

I wanted to make an impact. I am not happy with the mediocre. I really never did know what I wanted to "do" with my life. Even now I wonder how long I will stay in this phase. Whatever I do, or did, I strived at being the best. It was an internal struggle. Some of my best friends would tell me to relax and enjoy what I'm doing. But it was never that way for me. Some day I hope to learn how to relax.

My mother was a hard worker. She had to be. She married my stepfather, Howard Lyman, three years later and we moved to his farm and cattle ranch. I lived there until I went to college. They had two more children together and we grew up living the farm life: getting up early, feeding cows, cutting wheat, and cleaning out pig troughs. We knew what hard work was.

I left for college the day after high school graduation. I chose Montana State University though I don't know why. I just knew that I had to go to college and needed a college degree. I got the MSU curriculum and my choices were between engineering and nursing. I thought nursing would be easier, so that is what I chose.

I completed the four-year nursing program—but just barely. But that is not what counts. I learned to look at dead monkey's muscles, insert catheters and I.V.'s and assist with deliveries. I learned that making mistakes in this profession was life threatening. I learned about grams and grains, MS (that's morphine sulfate or Multiple Sclerosis), EKG's and EEG's. I learned quickly who knew more than I did, and I became their friend.

I landed my first nursing job in the Surgical Intensive Care Unit of Deaconess Medical Center in Billings, Montana. They had a serious nursing shortage and hired seven new-

Floret (detail)

grads that week. My big challenge was to keep my patients alive until the next crew came on and I was nervous and scared. It was a great place to work, and I made many friendships that still exist today. You experience something different working in critical care; there was a bond between the co-workers that I have never experienced working anywhere else.

Somewhere between the EKG's and EEG's of nursing school and the first job, I got married. The marriage lasted for ten years and we have two wonderful children, Jenna and Brandon. We both had different plans and were on different paths.

How does this all lead to the quilting stuff, you ask? Well, I took a night class, thinking that I would only make one quilt. Then I could say that I did that. Well, it turned into an addiction and an obsession-- a good one that is! The teacher wanted to be my friend, so I took another class from her and then I wanted to be her friend.

She encouraged me to open a quilt shop. I had two small kids, and was working in an obstetric department in a clinic. It was actually a great job, happy people, good hours...but I didn't feel challenged. I started buying fabric, and storing it in my basement for the grand opening of my shop, Fiberworks. I worked day and night making samples for the new shop. I was scared to death. I had it figured out just how many yards of fabric I would have to sell to pay the rent, and that was a nightmare. I opened the shop on January 2, 1994. I quit my nursing job January 3, 1994. I still keep my license active though. You never know what might happen.

Over the years, I have tried to learn from the adversities that came my way and to try to make something positive from the negative. I am very thankful to be able to have a profession where I can create and help other people create. It is very fulfilling to help customers and students learn to express themselves through quilting. To give of myself in this way is very rewarding.

Each of my quilts has a story. I will take you through my journey of self-expression. You will see the progression, and my movement towards more "color". This was not a planned thing, but rather an evolution for me, as it can be for you.

A poster on the wall of the dean's office at my daughter's school inspired me. It said, "Find what it is that interests you and that you can do well, and when you find it, put your whole soul into it." John D. Rockefeller III.

Now, as I write this book I realize that I am very lucky. I am doing what I enjoy and I have put my whole soul into it.

Dementia…n, 1996, collection of Linda Teufel

Color Fusion

Color fusion is the merging, melding and blending between the colors of the fabrics, the design and the threads combined. It is a layering process that can be done with the simplest of quilt patterns, fused fabric, and the play of thread on that fabric. Color fusion deals with the entire surface of the quilt. It begins with the base of the quilt and ends with the application of the binding. Each process that one goes through to complete the quilt is part of the color fusion. Different hues and values of colors interact to create an emotional reaction within us, of which we are often unaware.

The variety of texture, the feel of the threads and fabric, the richness of the surface and the intensity of color will all create a single "unity." I see everything around me in shapes and colors. Everything around us can be the start of a new quilt. I hope to share with you how color, whether it is in the fabric, thread, or embellishment, unites or "fuses" my world.

My color palette expresses my individual personality and outlook on life. Be guided by how you react to colors emotionally because your reactions can give you meaningful clues. Once you become open to and aware of the power of color, it will bring you grace and serenity. Color is like an instrument, and with practice you can learn to touch a particular nerve by combining—or "fusing"—certain chords of harmonious colors. Color instructs us to open our eyes and hearts to a wider vision. You can fuse colors together; creating your own color palette that should always be expanding to include the subtleties and mysteries of colors you like. There will be many colors in your life, and the more beautiful they are, the more glorious your happiness will be. Beautiful colors are the language of a radiant life.[1]

The Design

The design is an important part of the color fusion concept. The design should be fairly simple since the fabrics and thread choices will need to be considered also. If the design is too complicated, the entire quilt will be too busy.

The Fabrics

Choose fabrics that are unexpected. How about non-traditional fabrics for a traditional design? In your mind, picture the design in high value contrast fabrics and low value contrast fabrics to decide which works the best. Keep in mind that you still need to add the thread colors, which often will change the entire look of the quilt.

The Threads

You will need to think about thread types and colors during the process of choosing fabrics. Perhaps you have a quilting design that you love and really want it to show by using variegated threads. This will affect the fabrics that you choose. For example, you will not see a wonderful variegated thread on some print fabrics as well as you would on solid or mottled fabrics. The thread strongly effects the entire look of the quilt. A successful choice can unite—or fuse—the quilt design with the fabrics and the entire surface will transform.

[1] Stoddard, Alexandra, Alexandra Stoddard's Book of Color; 1998

Color Fusion

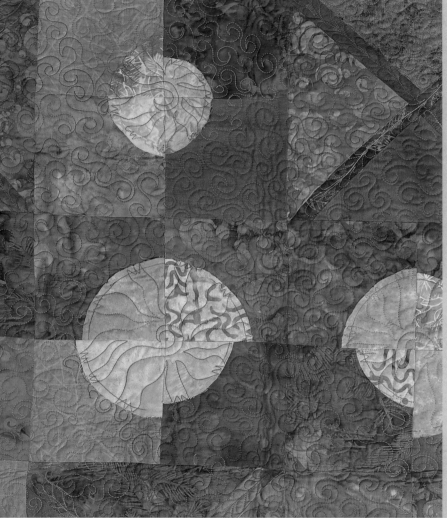

X's & O's, Kisses and Hugs (detail) quilted by Janet Caudill

One could broaden the Color Fusion term, applying it to the entire world around us. We are surrounded by colors in commercial settings that are meant to affect us psychologically. There are colors to stimulate hunger and happiness, colors to keep us awake and ones that will relax us. Dr. Taylor Hartman uses his "Color Code" book to describe different color personalities. His book helps people see the motives behind their own and other people's behavior as related to color[1].

People often ask me what my favorite color is. I have not one favorite color, but I love them all. My feeling is that in my quilting, as well as in my life, I need all the colors, because I like how they react with each other. My quilts, and my home, are full of colors, all different shades and values of each color. I mix reds with pinks, oranges with greens, dull colors with bright colors. I feel that in order for a color to be "pretty", it needs something not quite so "pretty" next to it. That way the pretty color is noticed. I have found that if a person says that she dislikes a color, it is probably because she does not know how to use it effectively. Challenge yourself with that color, use it and you may grow to appreciate it.

Using the Color Fusion process in this book, I will show you how easy it is to change the entire appearance of the quilt with the play of thread and embellishment. You will see that the simplest of designs can be transformed into true works of art.

[1] *Hartman, Taylor Dr.; Color Code; 1987*

My Background... early influences

I have had no formal art education. My degree is in nursing—the art of compassion. Friends tell me I have an ability to see color, and to choose fabrics that work well together. I don't know where this comes from. I think some people just have a natural instinct for color.

My mother tells stories about how I dressed myself when I was growing up. Knee-highs were in fashion when I was in grade school. I had a habit of putting on two different colored socks with my school dresses. One might be red and the other pink. I don't really remember this, but my mother has pictures to prove it! She would gently suggest that I needed to change one of my socks before I could leave for school. Now she says that I was trying to express my artistic self and that she might have suppressed my creativity. Thanks mom for NOT letting me go to school dressed like that!

I have significantly changed my tastes and ideas since childhood. Art class was always a challenge for me because you had to express yourself. I was somewhat shy. Even as I grew older, I avoided art classes. They made me feel too vulnerable.

As far as sewing, my grandmother taught me to hand stitch when I was young. We would sit together and make embroidered pillowcases when I visited her. She taught me all the basic stitches.

In junior high and high school, mom made my sister and I sew our own clothes. I hated everything I made, but this was mom's way of making us learn how to sew. She believed that all girls needed to have basic sewing skills.

I had this one shirt pattern with gathered cap sleeves. I knew how to make that pattern by heart. I bought ice cream cone appliqués, heart appliqués, every kind of appliqué there was, and put a different one on every shirt I made. Those shirts were all I wore. I didn't even hem the shirts since I always tucked them into my pants. Why waste your time with the hem if it was just going to be tucked in?

Darts were almost as bad. Why go through all those steps for a little dart? Needless to say, I got a 'C' in Home Economics. Even though my shirts were just fine without hems and darts, my teacher didn't think so! I was much better in the cooking series.

I did very little sewing during my college years. The only significant stitches I made were for deep cuts when assisting in surgery. Those took a special talent too!

Leftovers...12 years, 1997, 42.5" x 82"

I Made It... what I mean

I had packed his bags and placed them outside the house. I had changed the locks on the doors. He received the divorce papers that afternoon. While it seemed that I was living in a perfectly happy family, appearances can be deceiving. My self-confidence had eroded slowly through ten years of marriage; so slowly that I did not know it was happening. I had become a body molded into a different form.

Through my divorce, I discovered an inner strength that I did not know I had. I survived a seven-year custody battle and was able to withstand the probing eyes of court services, family services, psychologists, attorneys, psychiatrists, district court judges and supreme court judges. It was an ordeal that no one should have to endure. I am thankful to be standing on the other side.

I had a few things to empower me during those difficult years: my children, my friends, my business and my quilting. I knew I would never give up my children, no matter how long the battle continued or how costly the fight. I was prepared to sacrifice everything for them. Quilting became my salvation. It was my way to escape from the mess of my life. Each quilt captured a piece of the struggles I faced during those difficult years. Much of it is very personal-quilting was how I worked through the pain. I look back at some of those quilts, and wonder where all the ideas and energy came from? How did I produce such a massive number of quilts during a short period of time? I was driven by fear, the fear of not being able to "make it" through each day.

I searched every avenue for recognition in the quilting world. I entered competitions, designed patterns, wrote chapters, traveled, taught classes, signed on with a thread company, designed fabric and ran a quilt shop. I took on anything and everything to survive.

My friends were my sounding board. They provided me with unending support both personally and professionally. And the quilt shop became my new love. They say that you can be married to your business, and that is what happened to me. I nurtured my shop, fed it, and watched it grow. It was an unending source of energy for me. It revitalized me.

When I now say that "I Made It", it means that I was able to get through the hardships and succeed on my own. It means I discovered I had self worth. I could raise my two children as a single parent. I could walk out my front door with my head held high and be proud of my accomplishments, personally and professionally. I was able to turn a failed marriage into positive energy and production. It was a slow process. There were many days when I was depressed, but somehow a quilt in progress would call out to me. I would get up and put the final borders on a quilt, or go to work and get all my work done, so I could go home and quilt. Quilting was my therapy.

My compassion for people in emotional turmoil has deepened over time. As my own pain subsides, I see there are others who have endured far worse than I have. My experiences have made me a stronger, more empathetic person. And quilting has remained my obsession, my compulsion and my passion.

opposite page: Western Wear batik

Early quilts...and their stories

Beginning Sampler, 1986, 64" x 64"

My quilting journey began by making one quilt for my baby in a beginning quilting class. We learned how to make all kinds of different blocks, curved piecing, set-in seams, hand appliqué and basic templates. We were told to choose different fabrics, directionals, and large and small-scale prints.

This was difficult for me as I was pretty much a "Calico Sue". We only had one fabric store to choose from, unlike a quilt shop of today. It was a chain store, specializing in calicos and garment fabrics. I went to the store and picked all my rust and green fabrics. I stood there trying to decide what to buy. This was hard to do because we didn't even know what we were going to make! You got this supply list and you were on your own without any help from the sales ladies either. Their response was "You are making a what?"

Here I was, 24 years old, pregnant, and trying to do something that only "old" people do. What was the matter with me? Maybe I should cancel out of the class. I still have time; I can get my money back if I do it now. Oh what the heck. "Just buy the fabric and get on with your life", I told myself. Go to class, meet some old ladies and make your quilt. So I did.

The ladies that I met were not all "old". What is old anyway? The older I get, my view of what is old seems to get older. A few of us "younger" ones started a small quilt group. We met in each other's homes in the evenings since most of us worked day jobs.

Early quilts...and their stories

We also did fun things as a group. Each month we did a block exchange, where each member would make a block for you in your choice of pattern and colors. I chose an appliqué pattern and everyone loved me for it! *Star of Hearts* won honorable mention in a local quilt show. Winning added to my enthusiasm for quilting immensely!

Country Hearts and Homes was actually the second quilt that I made entirely by myself. I had taken some cheater cloth, cut out some people and their houses, added a border of flying geese around, and bound it. It was quick and simple. Our local art center had a quilt show every year, and I thought about entering it. The only problem was that it was 1" short of the size qualifications. So, I sewed a ruffle around the edge of the quilt. I entered the quilt and won first place in my category and I was so thrilled! It was later auctioned off so I am not sure who owns this quilt.

Scrap Kaleidoscope, 1988, 51" x 56"

Then, my beginning quilting teacher, Cheryl Wittmayer, who by now is my friend, said to me, "Laura, it is great that you won, but you were the only entrant in that category!" Well, that knocked the wind out of my sails! I didn't tell anyone else, and I hoped nobody else noticed it.

I started devouring quilting magazines, quilt books and finding out everything I could about quilting. Groups of friends continued to get together and quilt. Each time, we would work on a quilt for one member of the group. *Scrap Kaleidoscope* was made by a group of four friends. We just got together and stitched the day away.

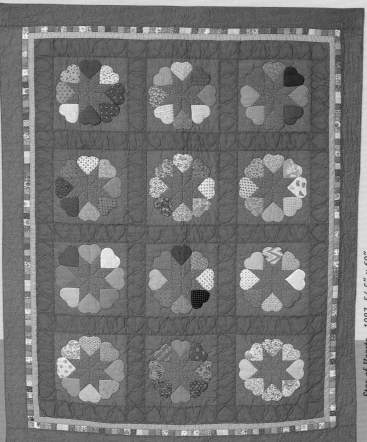

Star of Hearts , 1987, 54.5" x 69"

Roberta Horton's class in 1988 was a major turning point in my quilting development. We were to come to class with a pattern and large-scale prints. I didn't really like large-scale prints so I went to class with my favorites, which were basically all calicoes in blues and browns.

Roberta and I had trouble right off the bat! She sent me out at lunchtime to purchase large-scale prints. I questioned why I was doing this. I hated big prints. They were ugly! I didn't want to be doing this.

When I went back to class, with my four large-scale prints, she made me sew them into my basket pattern. The large scales would be the basket and my lovely calicos would be the backgrounds. This was as far as I could take it; but she wanted me to use some of my large scales for the background too. I just could not imagine this and she was pushing me over the edge!

So I began working…hating every minute of it and thinking that what I was doing was just awful. Well, I got two baskets done, and they didn't look so bad. In fact they actually looked much more interesting than the calico-with-calico combination. By the end of the day I was convinced that I did not have nearly enough large-scale prints to get the basket quilt done. I secretly went back to the store after class and bought more large-scale prints. I never told Roberta this, but this quilt was a very important lesson for me. I learned from actually doing, making myself do something I wouldn't ordinarily do, while fighting it all the way. It was a good lesson to learn.

Scrap Baskets, 1989, 33" x 44"

early quilts

Early quilts...and their stories

Maple Leaf , 1988, 56" x 56"

The big prints carried into my next quilts. I had forgotten some of what I learned about using the large-scale prints in the backgrounds when I made the **Maple Leaf** quilt. I could only bring myself to use them in the leaf sections of the quilt. Think of how much more interesting it would have been if I used them in the backgrounds too! But...look what I did on the back. This was new and innovative. Who would have thought at that time to piece the back too! I only did it to save on yardage for the backing fabric.

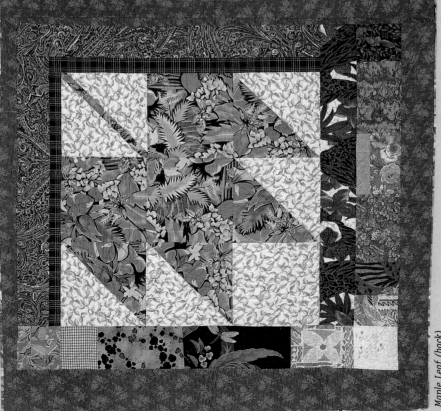

Maple Leaf (back)

Still in the brown, rust and green phase of my life, I thought I would try a curved pieced quilt. **Brandy Alexander** was made with the drunkard path pattern. It used one large-scale fabric and a hand-dyed looking background.

In 1988, we had a real quilt shop in town which was so exciting! As I was always looking for something new and challenging, I began to take an interest in Deirdre Amsden's quilts. She specialized in "colourwash" quilts. She was able to create illusion, transparency and three-dimensional effects with fabric. None of these words were familiar to me in relation to quilting and if I heard them I would not have understood them. I studied the thousands of fabrics that were used in her quilts. I realized that I needed more fabric and knew that each fabric needed to have action in it. In other words, it could not be my safe calicos. I couldn't believe that I was even thinking like this! Out with the calicos!

Brandy Alexander, 1989, 46" x 60"

Pinwheel Star, 1989, 60" x 60" collection of Mary Lou Palmer

My first attempt at colourwash was the **Pinwheel Star** quilt. I drew my design out on graph paper which was a first too. My friends were impressed. I put up a design wall in my unfinished basement and began cutting all my new fabrics into 2-1/2" squares, using seven hundred and twenty-four fabrics to be exact! This was a charm quilt too, where no two fabrics were alike. Lights were the backgrounds, the pinwheel star was the medium value and the squares were the dark values. Construction took forever. I learned a great lesson in color value during the process. I learned not to look at color, but the value of the fabric for its placement in the quilt. I hand-quilted it, entered it in a few shows and won third place in each one. A nursing friend, Mary Lou Palmer, purchased the quilt for $300 and it hangs in her home. It was the first quilt I ever sold.

As I looked at pictures of the finished quilt, or looked at the actual quilt from a distance, I could see where I could have improved it. I hadn't achieved the subtle "wash" look. My values started and stopped all at once instead of a more gradual shading of the values.

Hearts, 1990, 36" x 34", collection of Kay Wegner

Hearts developed from a quilt exchange that our local guild sponsored every year. Each person got a bag with somebody else's fabric in it, and you made something for that person. I drew out a pattern and continued with the colorwash technique. This quilt was much better than the first because my values had more of a gradual shading. Kay Wegner machine-quilted and owns this quilt.

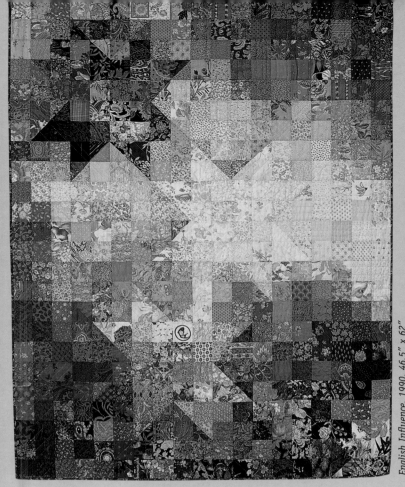

English Influence, 1990, 46.5" x 62"

A Rose is A Rose is A Rose, 1990, 70" x 80.5"

English Influence was entered in the 1990 American Quilter's Society Quilt Show and took third place in the Amateur Wall Quilt category. I was so excited, because the American Quilter's Society is one of the most prestigious competitions in the country. I just wanted to get accepted into the show and had no thought that I would ever win. I went to Paducah, Kentucky to accept my award and had the time of my life. I saw more quilts and quilt-related material than I could imagine. It was quilter's heaven and I was charged up to come home and create more wonderful quilts.

When I came home I buried myself in my quilting. It was a way for me to express myself, and achieve some sort of identity. I could hide within my quilts and move to a "better place".

A Rose is A Rose is A Rose was a quilt that I had thought about making for some time. A dozen long stem roses seem to lie on top of the quilt. It won People's Choice in a quilt show in Logan, Utah in 1993. I did not feel that the execution achieved quite what I was trying to do. It appeared too "stiff" to me. The colors did not flow as I had hoped. Sometimes I think that some quilts are just not possible. You may picture something in your mind, but in actuality, it is very hard to achieve. This was one of the few quilts that I hand quilted.

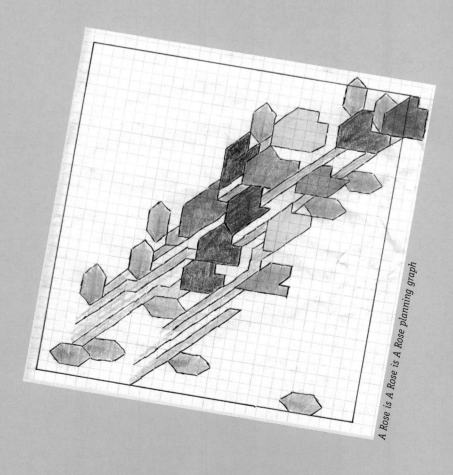

A Rose is A Rose is A Rose planning graph

My View of the World, 1991, 43" x 55"

early quilts

Early quilts...and their stories

Enter Nancy Crow. I took a three-day workshop with her in 1991. I really don't remember what the workshop was even about but I remember packing a large suitcase full of fabric, and a block that I had been working on. It was an interesting class. I began the class working with prints, blacks and whites, a little bit of red, and of course blue. Then I changed my mind and started a whole new quilt with solids and batiks and plaids. I didn't complete them in class, I only finished the blocks and took them home.

During the class, I asked Nancy to critique five of my finished quilts. Her response was that I had no direction. At the time I was very hurt since I thought that I knew where I was going. Later I could see that maybe what she was telling me was that I hadn't found a focus. I was still experimenting and learning about color and value. I can see this now, when I look back at my early quilts. In the workshop, I could not decide what I wanted to work with, thus two completely different quilts came from one person.

It was at this time that I realized I needed to learn from judges' comment sheets, and not to take them so personally. If I could do this, I would become a better quilter. For two years in a row, I received negative comments about my binding on quilts entered in large juried shows. So I took that information to heart, and learned how to make perfect binding. The information that Nancy Crow gave me was put in my memory bank. At that time there was probably nothing I could do about not having a "direction" in my quilting, but I vowed at some point I would change that.

Light From Within was one quilt made from the workshop with Nancy Crow. It was constructed with the plaid, solid and batik fabrics. It received the Best Use of Color award in a local museum quilt show. The remaining blocks were in a box, to be finished...who knows when?

Again, I went back to the watercolor technique. *My View of the World* was completed in 1991. I was trying to make an impressionistic view of row houses. I must have had it on my design wall for six months, almost giving up on it until a friend wanted to take it home with her in pieces. She said she would finish it. She liked it and I thought, if she liked it, then it must be good. This gave me enough of a push to finish it.

As I was piecing the top, I thought that if I appliquéd a lattice work over the top of the whole quilt, I could make the quilt look like the viewer was looking out of a window. When I did that, it added much more dimension. This quilt won an award wherever it was entered. Third place in the Wall Quilt category in the 1992 American Quilter's Society Show was the most prestigious award. This was one of the first quilts that I machine-quilted.

Light From Within, 1991, 32" x 39.5"

Early quilts...and their stories

Where Do You Live? was the second quilt in a series using houses as the design. This quilt was constructed with hand-dyed and solid looking fabrics. It was an impressionistic quilt, but using non-traditional impressionist fabrics. The backing fabric was an expensive hand-dyed fabric. I pieced a small section of the back so it would be large enough.

When the quilt was completely constructed, I showed it to a group of quilters. One of the quilters found a silhouette of a man and woman walking. It was in a pieced section in the quilt. I had not noticed this before! The quilt was machine quilted with metallic thread in a very tiny stipple. It was entered in numerous competitions and won first place in each one.

I had entered it in our State Fair quilt show. When I went to see the quilt on display, it was hung with the back facing out. It had received First Place and Judges' Choice, and both ribbons were hung on the back of the quilt! I thought that this was quite odd, but decided that if they liked the back better than the front then who was I to tell them that they couldn't judge the back! It was at this point in my quilting career that I decided that the back was just as important as the front!

Where Do You Live ? (detail of man and woman walking)

Where Do You Live? (front), 1991, 45.5" x 55"

Where Do You Live ? (back)

Early quilts...and their stories

Remember the blocks from the Nancy Crow class that I threw in a box? Well, I pulled them out and stuck them on my design wall. I placed them on the wall with the print blocks on the top and the plaid and batik blocks on the bottom. I just did this to get all the blocks up on the wall. I had planned on making two different quilts. When I stood back to look at all the blocks, I could see that they all blended together. It was unbelievable and so unplanned. The two different quilts were sewn together joined at the fifth horizontal row, and the quilt was called *Best of Both Worlds*. It was machine quilted with a tiny stipple in metallic thread. It received many awards, one of which was the Award of Excellence in the Art Quilt category in the American International Quilt Association's contest in 1992.

Best of Both Worlds , 1991, 39.5" x 73.5"

Betrayed (detail)

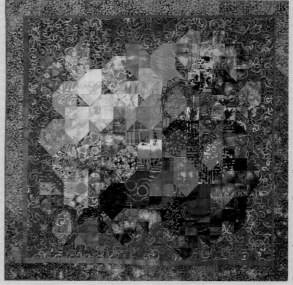

Betrayed, 1991, 57" x 54"

Well, we all have done a therapy quilt or two, haven't we? I think all of mine were therapy quilts! As a friend of mine had told me, I can get inside my quilts and just stitch my life back together. **Betrayed** was just that quilt for me. It started out as a happy quilt with different people's faces, but soon was turned into a jumbled mess of betrayal. I had trusted someone, who ended up hurting my family. It seemed that I didn't really know that person at all. At the time, I felt like I probably didn't really know anyone at all. The faces in the quilt became confused, and mixed up. They were there, but you just couldn't really see who they were. I haven't shown this quilt much to anyone. It was only a process that helped me get through a bad time. It has no real purpose now.

Early quilts...and their stories

About this time, my group of guild girlfriends decided that they wanted to start hand-dyeing fabric. Well, when you want to do it, it is NOW! The only dye that we could get our hands on was Rit Dye at the grocery store so we bought all they had. Then we needed muslin. Any kind would do so we got that dollar-per-yard stuff and bought bolts of it! We tried to dye in gradations and with trial and error, it sort of worked.

Plaids to Dye For came out of this dyeing frenzy. It was a class that I took with my beginning quilting teacher using the cathedral window quick method. This quilt was just plain fun to do and hangs in my office today.

Plaids to Dye For (back)

Plaids to Dye For, 1992, 44" x 44"

Plaids to Dye For (detail)

How Does Your Garden Grow? (detail)

How Does Your Garden Grow?, 1992, 64" x 73.5"

Our local quilt shop, in conjunction with the American International Quilt Association, ran a quilt contest statewide called the *Labor of Love* contest. It consisted of a local shop contest, which you had to enter first. You were required to buy 75% of the fabrics for your quilt at the local shop, make a quilt and enter it in the local contest. The winner from each shop would then have their quilt entered in the larger American International Quilt Contest in Houston.

This sounded like a lot of fun! I thought about what I would do for a long while. I wanted to win of course, and from my experience I determined that people seemed to like the watercolor quilts and since the winner was chosen by people's choice, this was important. So, I proceeded to do another watercolor quilt.

The local quilt shop was small. I went in the shop and purchased quarter yard cuts of every floral fabric that they had. I started to make the quilt and soon became frustrated. I didn't have enough colors and values to get a good gradation. How could I do this without buying a whole bunch more fabrics from another store and getting disqualified?

So, that's where the dyeing became helpful! I went to the grocery store again, and bought some more Rit Dye. I also bought the color remover, thinking that I would need to remove some color to achieve the very light values. I set up a little color lab in my studio and it worked! I dyed, over-dyed, bleached and also used the backs of the fabrics from that store. **How Does Your Garden Grow?** was completed in 1992. It was completely pieced, including the latticework. Machine quilting was done with monofilament thread and a tiny stipple stitch. It won the local quilt show, and traveled to the International Quilt Festival to win Best of Show! It was truly a labor of love. As I look at it today, I am amazed by it and wonder how I did it.

Early quilts...and their stories

If I could do a watercolor quilt with prints then why couldn't I do it with plaids? Now this was a challenge. *I Valued My Plaids* was an attempt at plaid colorwash. It was difficult to do because most plaids have both light and dark values within them, and many colors. I went to my friend Sandi's house and dug through her plaid stash. I looked for every plaid imaginable. I even went to the thrift stores and bought old plaid clothing. There was one pink vintage summer jumpsuit that I cut up, put in the quilt and it will live on forever.

This quilt was machine quilted in a zigzag stitch, entered in a few shows, but never won. I learned from it though. If you want a challenge in value gradation, just work with plaids!

Monet's House, 1993, 59.5" x 73", collection of Margaret Nybo

I Valued My Plaids, 1992, 57.5" x 71"

My quilting studio had been in our basement for years. There are no windows in this basement. I found it truly exciting to bring a finished top from the basement upstairs and see how vibrant the colors were, so different than how they appeared downstairs. I had the entire finished basement to myself, and I enjoyed it down there. I often wondered if I could make a quilt in daylight.

After my ex-husband moved out, I moved my quilt studio upstairs. I decided that I needed the light. I moved back to the technique that I thought I knew well-watercolor with traditional watercolor fabrics. I needed a diversion. I couldn't come up with a pattern on my own, so I chose a Monet painting to replicate.

Monet's House, completed in 1993, was a reflection of his painting *Monet's House in Argenteuil*. My colors were not exactly right, and it was again somewhat "stiff". Why did I use black for the overhanging tree branches? Why not a dark green? I decided only later that it was the best that I could do at the time.

Margaret Miller came to town, and I still needed a diversion from my personal troubles, so I took Margaret's class, Strips That Sizzle. We were to bring about five different fabrics in two to three different colorways. Once again, I couldn't just bring fifteen different fabrics. I brought a whole suitcase of all kinds of different colors. My strips sizzled all right! **Opposing Forces** started as a fight against warm and cool colors and once the batik face mask panels were put in, it became a fight against good and evil. Our divorce was beginning its long trail of agony and it surfaced in this quilt.

Opposing Forces, 1993, 60.5" x 70"

Opposing Forces (detail)

Early quilts...and their stories

For some reason, fish became a focus. Next, I designed a simple fish pattern, blew it up, stretched it and made this huge quilt called *One Fish, Two Fish, Red Fish, Blue Fish!* It was just massive. The American Quilter's Society competition was coming up, and I just happened to look at the size qualifications. This quilt was way too big for any category.

I decided to take pleats in the back of the quilt going in both directions until the quilt fit into the largest category. Can you believe that? I started pleating away. The front of the quilt ended up quite interesting, as it appeared that it was template pieced, when it had actually been paper pieced. No seams matched, and the fish looked as if they were swimming through water, somewhat distorted, as water would do.

The quilt was machine quilted with a seaweed pattern in the background and each fish had something different quilted within his body. It finished at 83" wide by 93" long. I wish I had saved the measurements before I did all the pleating! I filled out an entry blank for the contest and was later notified that it was accepted!

Meanwhile, I opened a quilt shop. Basically, just like that. I took a trip with the same quilt friends and they talked me into this endeavor! I was busy running the shop when I got a call from Klaudeen Hansen from American Quilter's Society. It appears that they hadn't received my quilt, and judging was tomorrow. They suggested that I check with UPS to try to track my quilt.

"No need to do that...it is still hanging on my wall at the quilt shop. I am looking at it now." I couldn't believe that I forgot to mail it. I asked her how I could get it there in time. The only chance would be Federal Express, and that was a long shot. Paducah, Kentucky is a small town, with small airlines going in, and it just might not

One Fish, Two Fish, Red Fish, Blue Fish!, 1993, 83" x 93", collection of American Quilter's Society

make it. I packaged it up and took it to Federal Express. The bill was $52.00! I still remember this. I remarked to one of my friends, that I couldn't believe that I was spending $52 to ship a quilt to a show! I was so disgusted with myself that I would have spent more. It was such an honor alone to be accepted and then I forget to mail the quilt!

The next day came, and I called the "quilt head-quarters" to see if they got the quilt. They didn't know but they would check and get back to me. I didn't hear anything that day. The next day I got a call from Klaudeen Hansen. They received the quilt and I had won the Bernina Award! Wonderful! I was in the middle of teaching a class so I told Klaudeen to send the quilt back to the shop rather than my house after the show. She paused and said, "OK."

I returned to my class to tell them that I won the Bernina award for Best Machine Workmanship. They all asked, "Well how much money is that award?" I didn't know. I had the entry form in my office and I would run down at lunch to find out. Lunch came and I nearly had a heart attack! I dug out the entry form to find that I had won $10,000 cash and that the quilt would hang in the AQS quilt museum. Or, the other option was that I could take my quilt back! Well, I had just told Klaudeen Hansen to ship my quilt back to my shop. Did she think that I didn't want the money? Needless to say, the class was history after that. I called Klaudeen back and she just laughed. She had suspected that I didn't understand what I had won.

It couldn't have come at a better time. My shop could use that $10,000 boost. I really couldn't believe it. What was so great about that quilt? My biggest fear was trying to improve on that award in the future. Best machine workmanship. Wow! What would or could I do next? Was this the end? Should I not try to compete internally with myself? Relax, I kept telling myself. But I would not listen.

Cabbage Rose, 1994, 47" x 67"

Latest quilts...and their stories

Cabbage Rose (detail)

Over the next few years I continued to make quilts, but my focus was more with the shop. I made many shop samples, using other people's patterns and designs. I had to have samples in the shop in order to sell patterns and fabric. It was a time-consuming business and I found that out early. I discovered that my customers wanted exactly what they saw, which meant that you needed to be continually sewing new samples. I slowed down on the art quilts for one reason, they took so much time, and another reason, I was afraid of not "winning." I had an excuse for not producing art quilts...I was busy with the shop.

I still got together with my quilting friends though not as often and the friends changed. **Cabbage Rose** was made with two of my dear friends, Cheryl Wittmayer, my first teacher, and Lisa Harris. We just got together one day and worked on a quilt for me, followed by quilts for both of them. It was a day of "no-brain" work. I needed this once in awhile. It was machine-quilted with variegated thread, never entered in a show, but is just a very special quilt that continues to hang in my home.

Most of the quilts that I did during this time revolved around a class. I felt that I needed to make a quilt that would inspire someone to take a class. *Purple Kaleidoscope* quilt was a class sample. I taught many a student how to make kaleidoscope quilts. They were fun and fast, and a successful quilt for beginners. Then I started to get crazy with the concept using a lot of wild fabrics in my quilt shop that most people were afraid to use.

Purple Kaleidoscope, 1994, 54" x 64"

I cut yardage from all of the bright wild fabrics that didn't sell, took them home and sewed up a kaleidoscope quilt using every last one of them. I proved to my students and myself that you could do a kaleidoscope quilt successfully with tons of random fabrics! You just needed to get the value right in the fabric placement. And...I had lots of experience with value placement. It was machine quilted with all kinds of different threads, and embellished with cross-locked beads. *Kaleidoscope Krazy* was entered in the local quilt show at the museum and it received Best of Show and First Place in the Art category. Wow...I did it! I could actually win again. So off it went to Houston for the American International Quilter's Association Quilt Show where it received the Award of Excellence. It was also placed on the cover of the quilt show brochure. You can't imagine the relief that I felt.

Kaleidoscope Krazy, 1994, 92.5" x 71"

latest quilts

I came back home from the show and a buying trip for the shop, needing a break. I was pretty busy with the kids, the shop, and just life in general. I wanted to quilt, but had no ideas. I was tired of doing shop samples with other people's designs, but had no original ideas of my own. I remembered the *Maple Leaf* quilt that I had done, thought about how I could improve upon it, so started to work on another one.

I remembered that I should have used prints with more action in them for the backgrounds, so it wouldn't have been so boring. I created **Falling Leaves**, with this in mind. My backgrounds were mainly hand-dyed fabrics, but busy ones. My leaves were all leftover plaids from the *I Valued My Plaids* quilt...yes, even the vintage plaid jumpsuit is in this one too. I moved the blocks around, so each leaf was not going in a planned pattern and I braided the border. Don't ask me where this came from. Look how much more interesting this quilt became! It was machine quilted by Vi Russell, never entered in a show, and continues to hang in my home.

Falling Leaves, 1994, 58.5" x 69.5"

Big Fish; Small Pond, 1994, 87" x 76" collection of Beverly and Gary Young

So now I am into this phase of improving upon my old quilts. How about the fish? I know I could have done better there. Or am I playing with fire? It already won one of the top awards, how could I top that? I'll try.

Big Fish; Small Pond was completed start to finish in three months. I took the same fish pattern from *One Fish, Two Fish, Red Fish, Blue Fish*, made it tiny, and made dozens of fish. The background was tough to do. There is a superimposed big blue fish in the background, made with the value placement of the background fabrics. Each fish was quilted in its own special way. Many different kinds and colors of threads were used. I planned this one, and didn't have to sew the pleats in the back of the quilt! It finished at 87 inches wide by 76 inches long—just 4" short of size requirements for the AQS show. Maybe this was meant to be.

I entered it anyway. Do they actually measure them? Well, the answer is yes. Klaudeen Hansen called me again but not to tell me that she had not received the quilt this time, but rather to tell me that my quilt was not big enough! Can you believe it? Not big enough this time. If I had sewn my rod pocket on the other way, it would work size-wise, but the fish would be swimming straight up in the air. "Sorry," she said. It can't even hang in the show. So, don't do it. Don't even waste your time because they will measure them.

Instead it went to the American International Quilter's Association Quilt show in Houston. It fit within their size requirements. It received the Award of Excellence in the 1995 show. But I decided—no more fish quilts.

Field Of Flowers was a quilt from an American School of Needlework book by Donna Wilder. It had great flowers, and was really cheerful. I wanted to use fun, vibrant fabrics, and I used lots of threads, beads and button embellishments. The flowers were fused, because this was much faster than hand appliqué.

I couldn't do satin stitch machine appliqué very well and didn't want to do hand appliqué, so I decided to do some free motion thread work instead. When I did this quilt, I really didn't know what I was doing. I was just securing the fused flowers to the background with free motion sewing. This must have been something rather new because people were just intrigued by it. It looked really hard to do but it was actually quite easy, and it used lots of thread. That was good for shop sales.

Field of Flowers (detail), 1995, 56" x 70"

I had purchased the whole line of Sandy Gervais' *Piece of My Heart* collection for the shop. This was a first for me. I was a new shop owner, small and scared. I decided that I probably should do something to get customers involved with the fabrics so I would be assured that this big investment would sell. I created a challenge with her fabric line. I had to make a quilt too, to get their interest going, so I made **A Piece of MY Heart**. It was my design of a heart with a star inside of it. All the small hearts form a large heart, which is incomplete, and this was where the title came from. It was a great quilt show, and I ended up selling all of the fabric!

A Piece of MY Heart, 1995, 27" x 76"

The Liberty of London fabrics that I purchased a year and a half before were still sitting in the shop looking pretty and getting dusty. They were too expensive to just sit there, so...back to the colorwash quilts. **Trip to London** was made from a *Piecemakers Colorwash Trip Around the World* book. This was a great way for customers to make a colorwash quilt without purchasing tons of fabrics. The inside of the quilt was constructed completely with Liberty of London fabrics and the outer border was a batik. It proved that you could mix batiks with florals and it worked.

Trip to London, 1995, 60" x 69"

My Aunt Arlene moved to my town. She was a talented watercolor artist although she did not consider herself to be one. I had a collection of glass bottles in a bay window of my home that she would photograph and then paint. I would listen to her talk about transparency as she painted.

The thought occurred to me to do a quilt using the bottles. As inspiration I took a photo of the bottles and made a line drawing of them using grid paper, like I did for the colorwash quilts. I started cutting up 2-1/2" squares and putting them up on my design wall. The individual bottles were easy to do, but when they overlapped and the colors mixed, it became challenging. Fabric choice was difficult since I needed to find fabric colors that appeared to be transparent.

 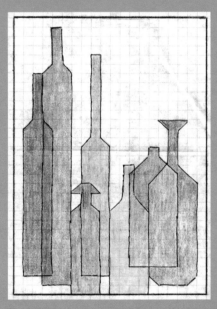

I found a fairy in Sharon Yenter's new line of fabrics for *In the Beginning*. The fairy was perfect, and it would fit into one of the bottles. I asked Sharon for her permission to draw her fairy, replicate it in thread and place it inside one of the bottles. So the fairy was trapped in the orange bottle. The quilt was titled **Bottled.**

With the top completed, I was off to Quilt Market. My mom joined me this time and we had a great time. During my last day of shopping we happened across a booth filled with all kinds of different threads. There was a man standing in the booth, looking tired, as we all were, and ready to pack up and go home. I was feeling sort of chipper and asked him what he was selling. "Thread," was his reply. I

asked him about his thread, what size needle to use with his thread, how should I use it, and most importantly, why didn't he have any quilts in his booth? We were actually at a quilt market you know. His response was, "Why don't you make me a quilt for my booth?". Yeah, right. Everyone wants someone to make them a quilt! He gave me a whole sack of thread and sent me on my way. I had no idea how to use some of the threads that he packed up for me. I wondered if he knew!

I went home, unpacked all my "stuff", and threw the sack of "thread" on my quilting table. The spools rolled and landed right by the *Bottled* quilt top. I stopped for a moment to look at what I saw. This man had given me the most wonderful thread! It was a heavy variegated thread that matched the quilt top it was laying next to perfectly! I opened the spool of thread. It was so thick. What needle should I use? I called the company. Surely they would know. No, they were not sure—maybe a universal needle? Good answer!

It was YLI Jeans Stitch thread and the needle to use is a 90/14-machine embroidery. I quilted like a crazy woman with this thread. Twenty-one hundred yards of thread to be exact. It was the coolest stuff I had ever seen and it did great things to the quilt! I finished the quilt, and sent it to this man, Lanny Smith, president of YLI. Less than a week later, he called me on the phone. It was a good thing that I had taken a picture of it before I sent it, because it never came back. They purchased the quilt and used it for their ads and brochures. This began my relationship with YLI.

I would bring my quilts to Quilt Market and Lanny would display them in his booth. I watched his company soar before my eyes. I used his threads on my quilts. People would see it and want it, especially Jeans Stitch. It was such a different thread, very heavy and thick and added quite a touch to the quilts. I became an educator for YLI and I taught for them at Quilt Market seminars. The relationship was great for both of us.

Bottled, 1996, 59.5" x 63.5", collection of YLI.

Crown Royal, 1996-2001, 18" x 65" & 42.5" x 65"

On one of these trips back from the Houston Quilt Market I met a man on the airplane. He just happened to be going all the way to Billings, Montana to do some hunting. He traveled a lot, and liked to have a good time wherever he went. He found out that I was a quilter, and sent me a huge box of Crown Royal bags. He had been collecting them for (I hope) a lifetime. There were at least 150 of them, in all different sizes too. He didn't know what to do with them. He figured that I could make a "blanket" out of them. Oh, great. We quilters love to make blankets. This was completely out of my ballpark. I had no idea what to do with them, other than to give one to each of my friends. I still had dozens left so decided to make a quilt.

The **Crown Royal** quilt was made with 31 of the bags in the large quilt and six bags in the small quilt. It is actually two different quilts, and when they hang side-by-side the heart that forms with the crown royal bags is complete. The design was a spin off from the *Piece of MY Heart* quilt. It was quilted with yellow Jeans Stitch in the heart section and purple Jeans Stitch in the background. This was a fun quilt, but I never did anything with this one. Just like the guy, I guess. It was made in two parts to signify the distance between us, and that the two of us would probably never get together.

Dementia...n, 1996, 47" x 62", collection of Linda Teufel

Custody battles, Court Services, Family Services, Psychologists, Attorneys of the drawn-out divorce led me into ***Dementia...n***. Talk about a jumbled up quilt of confusion, this was it. This quilt was completed in July of 1996. It was a difficult period for me. I felt that the quilt was a total failure as far as concept and design were concerned, but it helped me through a period of personal turmoil.

This quilt, for me, was "crazy"—just how I felt at the time, hence the name dementia. If you add the "n" to the end of the name, the word sounds like "dimension" which describes the trapunto in the quilt.

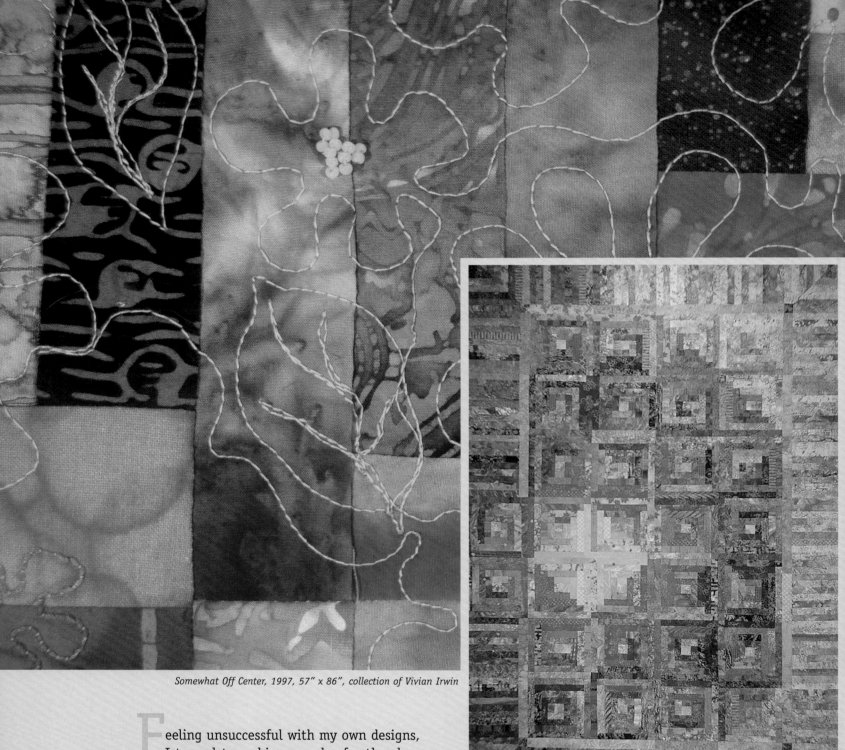

Somewhat Off Center, 1997, 57" x 86", collection of Vivian Irwin

Photo by Tilton

Feeling unsuccessful with my own designs, I turned to making samples for the shop again. Cindy Edgerton was designing quilting patterns for McCall's and I chose her paper pieced log cabin quilt to make for the shop. I thought it would be a great quilt for beginners. Her quilt on the cover of the pattern was very traditional. I believe the colors were basically all browns and creams. I decided to do mine in bright vibrant colors. I began piecing the blocks and putting them on my design wall. I discovered that I liked the quilt better if the "center" of the quilt was actually pulled off to the side. It made the quilt look very contemporary, even though it was a simple log cabin design.

Somewhat Off Center was completed in 1997. It received second place in the Pacific Northwest Quilt Show in 1998 in the Traditional Quilt category. It seemed to baffle everyone who looked at it. It was quilted with a variegated Jeans Stitch thread in the bobbin, using the backing fabric for the quilting design. The Jeans Stitch thread in the bobbin actually shows on the top of the quilt.

A Native American friend of mine, Jerry Belgarde, makes star quilts. She has made more star quilts than she can count. I thought it would be a great idea if she pieced a star quilt top and I did the quilting. We could enter it in our local museum quilt show as a two-person quilt. She did such a wonderful job of making these quilts that I just had to have one for my personal collection. I picked out the fabrics and she made the star quilt top.

Jerry explained to me that if the star is done "right," it bursts. It will burst if you use the background fabric, or one of the same values as the background, in the offshoot point sections of the star. I quilted it in variegated Jeans Stitch thread, in a small square stipple pattern. We entered it in the show and won third place in the group category! *Jerry's Star* is a great quilt, with dynamic use of color.

Jerry's Star, 1996, 63" x 63"

51

At this point, I had been quilting for 12 years. It was hard for me to believe that I had sustained this passion for so long. I had many quilts that were unfinished, as we all do, and many quilts that were only one block big. I had an idea to take all of the blocks that I had leftover from the last 12 years and see if I could sew them together to make a quilt. I pulled them all out of their hiding places and placed them on my design wall. It was unbelievable how the colors all fit together. They didn't look half bad. They were all different sizes, so I had to be pretty creative in order to get them all put together and end up with a squared quilt. *Leftovers* was completed in 1997. It was heavily machine quilted with YLI cotton and Jeans Stitch thread. It had so many memories! It was so much fun to do, and to look at even today. It won third place in the International Quilt Festival in 1997.

Leftovers...12 years, 1997, 42.5" x 82"

My children spent most of the summer of 1997 with their father. They left and I heard nothing for almost sixty days. No phone calls. No letters. Nothing! This was not unusual, but it was very hard. When they left, I started a quilt with the three of us, our silhouettes, jumping rope together. It was a watercolor quilt again. I wanted it to be "pretty", which is why I chose the watercolor technique.

It took me all of the sixty days to cut the fabrics out and get them placed properly in the quilt. The more I worked on it, the more I missed the children and wondered how they were doing. **We Three** was completed in the fall of 1997 after the children were home. elinor peace bailey came to teach at the shop in 1998. She saw the quilt hanging and asked who had made it. She was surprised to hear that I had. Her comment was "The colors are so dark, what is the matter with you? Are you depressed?"

You have to know elinor to know that she calls it how she sees it. I don't know if "depressed" was the right word. Maybe it was. Whatever it was, it sure came out in this quilt. I really did try to use lots of color. This quilt was another that I quilted upside down, using the backing fabric as the quilting design. You can see the backing fabric on the far right side.

We Three, 1997, 71.5" x 67.5"

53

I was asked by a fabric company, Kings Road, to be part of a color challenge. A few shops were chosen to complete a small quilt with one colorway of their new fabric collection. I really don't know why I was chosen. I liked the company because they had "different" fabrics. My first Quilt Market was also their first Quilt Market, and they always remembered that. They would remind me of that each year that I would stop at their booth to buy fabric; we were both still hanging in there!

I was given the pink colorway. Of all the colors in the world, why did I get pink? The rule was that you had to use all of the prints in your quilt. They even sent some silk and wool along that coordinated with the fabric line. Wow! What in the world was I going to do? I had never used silk or wool before in my life! It had to be great because it would hang at the next Quilt Market, and be judged by us, the fabric buyers!

Pretty in Pink was made using every different piece of fabric that they sent. The wool was machine appliquéd in the corners of the quilt and the silk was the heart appliqué. All of the fabrics in the collection were pieced for the background. I won second place and guess which color won first? Blue. The blue quilt was beautiful. So began my relationship with Kings Road Imports.

Pretty in Pink, 1997, 28.5" x 28.5"

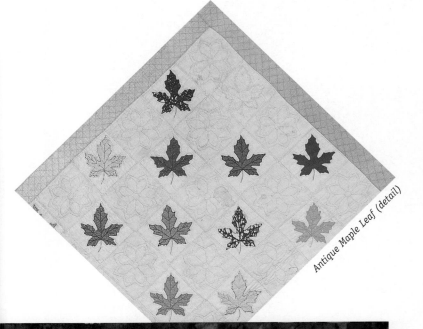

After Market, I took a weekend off and went out of town to go antique shopping. I found this old leaf quilt literally in shreds. It had a price tag of $25.00 on it. It looked so helpless, thrown over the door of a cupboard. It had holes completely worn through it. I loved the pattern so I bought it. It gave me inspiration. It cost me two hundred and fifty dollars to repair the quilt, but it was worth every penny.

From that quilt, I designed *Turning Over a New Leaf*. It actually came at a turning point in the ongoing divorce saga. We had recently been to court, and our battle was pretty much at the end. The judge granted us joint custody with the children primarily residing with me and my ex-husband getting visitation. I worked on this quilt as I worked on preparing for the court battle. When it was over, I felt freed.

This quilt was by far my most successful challenge. Every quilter who designs patterns dreams of having just one successful pattern. It will put you over the edge. This was mine.

I gave the pattern to YLI. Lanny designed the cover and marketed it for me. I had no idea it would be a showstopper. It won Judges' Choice in the International Quilt Association Quilt Show in 1998.

Turning Over a New Leaf, 1998, 64" x 64" Photo by Tilton (collection of Hiroko Yachi)

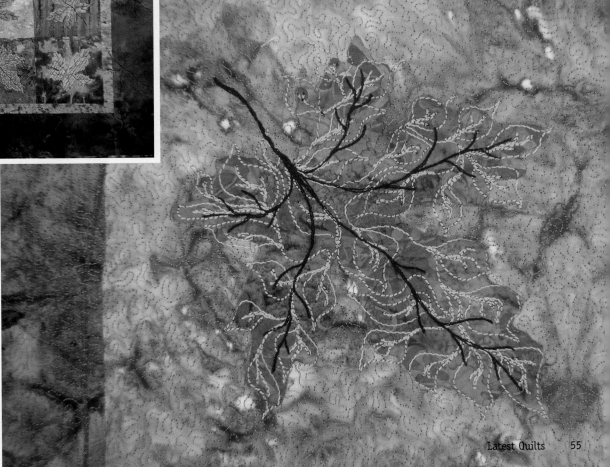

Photo by Tilton

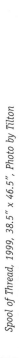

Spool of Thread, 1999, 38.5" x 46.5", Photo by Tilton

Spool of Thread stained glass by Dione Roberts

*Cider House Blooms,
1999, 34" diameter.
Stained glass by
Dione Roberts*

My friend, Dione Roberts, owns a stained glass shop and I commissioned her to make a stained glass window of my logo for Fiberworks. She is the most wonderful glass artist that I know! When I saw her design on paper in her shop I said, "Oh, I need to make a quilt like that, it would be so wonderful!" Her response was, "Do it!"

She gave me the design on paper, and we each worked independently, not knowing what the other was doing. The deal was that if I did one of Dione's patterns I had to make two. She had a beautiful round glass piece titled *Cider House Blooms*. She really wanted me to reproduce it in fabric. It was much harder to do because it was round. I love the quilt and it fits under glass on my dining room table. It was trapunto'd and machine embellished. It is a special quilt for me because I used the first line of fabrics that I designed and each color-way is represented in the quilt. This quilt for me symbolizes a treasured friendship that I have with Dione. She is such a wonderful artist and I was honored to be able to share her work.

Paper Dolls (detail) "Jeanine"

Husqvarna Viking sent me a loaner sewing machine with the embroidery unit. With it came a card of elinor peace bailey's faces to embroider. I had fun with these faces and designed a paper doll pattern to use with them. **Paper Dolls** was a great quilt. The children in our family each made a block. I sewed them together for a **Family** quilt. We gave it to my mom and stepfather for their birthdays, which happen to fall on the same day.

left, Jeanine. right, Laura

Paper Dolls, 1998, 45" x 76"

58   Color Fusion

Flowers and Flies, 1998, 56.5" x 79"

Block-of-the-Month had become popular in the quilting industry. Everyone was doing at least one. So I decided I needed to design one, too. I wanted mine to be different. I began drawing flower patterns, and started to write a story about a garden.

Each block or flower's story had to tie into the next one to keep the interest going, and one had to get all twelve patterns to find out how the story ended. I had so much fun that I had the story completed before all the blocks were designed. This quilt didn't take very long to complete but it totally consumed me. Each block averaged eight hours from start to finish which included fusing, cutting, machine embroidery, trapunto, quilting and outline stitching. *Flowers and Flies* was finished in three months time. YLI used the quilt for their ads for quite some time.

Divine Inspiration was made especially for my mother. It depicts my three sisters and myself. The blocks are quite large, and were hand buttonhole-stitched by my friend Wanda Nelson. She wore through many thimbles in the process. My mother, with her own designs, embellished each angel with silk ribbon.

The quilt was used by YLI in their ads. It was on the back cover of Quilter's Newsletter Magazine for so many issues that I have lost count. We won third place in the International Quilt Association Quilt Show in 1999 in the group category. It was fun and memorable to receive an award with my mother.

Divine Inspiration, 1999, 60.5" x 92", collection of Willow Lyman

Look At My Wings, 1999, 50" x 52"

Look At My Wings was designed for a class that I was teaching at the shop. The class was an angel sampler. The students learned a different technique every month for a six-month period. I needed a new technique for this class, and designed this pattern. The wings of the angels were made with thread, and were dimensional. The lacemaking looks difficult but is actually quite easy.

Folk Art Flowers and Flies was a work in a series stemming from the *Flowers and Flies* quilt. In this quilt, the patterns were much easier and the pieces were larger with more of a "folk art" look. I had the top pieced and fused, started the machine embroidery, and then life took over. I found myself busy with designing new lines of fabric and making samples of the prior fabric collection that I designed. I just could not get back to this quilt. Everything was on a timeline and I wasn't going to make it. I really wanted to get the quilt entered in some shows and the pattern completed. I couldn't get the pattern completed until the quilt was finished and photographed. By now, my mother had been traveling with me quite often to Quilt Markets, sitting in on many classes, and could just about replicate what I did. She finished the machine embroidery work for me. I machine quilted the quilt and we entered it in the International Quilt Association Show in 2000 in the group category. It didn't win an award, but I did receive a phone call from Oxmoor House/Leisure Arts. Patricia Wilens, the editor of *Great American Quilts* was interested in the story about the quilt and wanted to feature it in their next book!

Folk Art Flowers and Flies, 2000, 80" x 80"

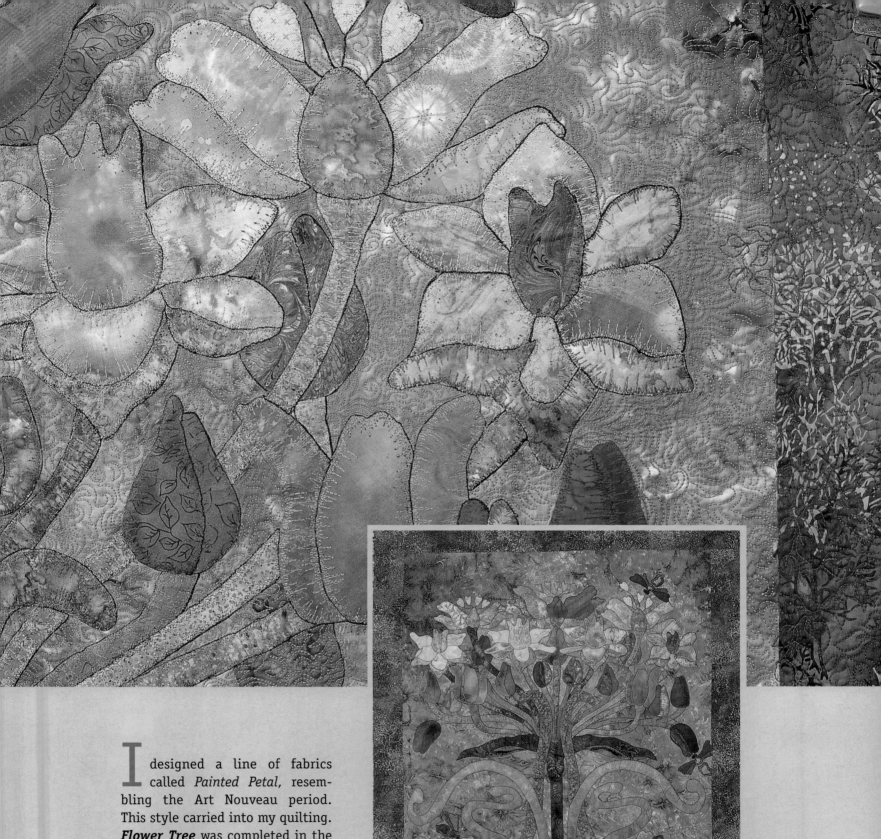

I designed a line of fabrics called *Painted Petal,* resembling the Art Nouveau period. This style carried into my quilting. **Flower Tree** was completed in the fall of 2000. It was an adaptation of actual works in the Art Nouveau style. I was searching for something new and different. It had to be happy and beautiful and free. It represented my life at that stage... complete!

Flower Tree, 2000, 52.5" x 74.5"

Photo by Tilton

Fiberworks...the store

With a small cash settlement from my divorce, I decided to take the plunge and open the store in January 1994. My choices were to try the shop, or continue to be a nurse. I liked the idea of "making my own hours" since I had two small children, and figured this would be better for us all. Little did I know what was ahead of me! It was probably a good thing that I didn't or I probably never would have done it.

I had 1,500 square feet, with 350 feet dedicated as classroom space. It was in a prime location, on one of the main streets in Billings. I paid a premium rent for the spot. It was a new building, so the owners basically fixed it up as I wished. I began collecting fabric and storing it in my home about six months prior to opening. Shipping dates on fabric are so unpredictable so I had to do this to ensure a decent selection of fabric on opening day.

I opened on January 2nd with 800 bolts of fabric and a fairly good selection of notions, books and patterns, or so I thought. My shelves were not quite full, but I tried to make them look good. I had a fair number of samples to help make the shop look inviting. There was great support from quilters locally and from the surrounding states. My newsletter went out right away, offering classes, demos and coupons.

Every bit of money that flowed into the shop, I tried to leave there. I took very little money home to live on. I survived on my savings for about three years. These were very hard and it was more time-consuming than I had thought. I did the basic accounting work, payroll and accounts payable myself and computerized the entire inventory of the store. There were three part-time employees who helped me in the beginning.

fiberworks

Fiberworks...the store

Meanwhile, I never turned down any opportunities that came my way. I began designing patterns and promoting thread for a thread company. I wrote chapters for books and articles on quilting for magazines and newspapers. I promoted myself as a teacher and started traveling and teaching throughout the United States. I knew that I would need to do more than just open my doors to be successful in my new chosen career. I made many mistakes, but learned from each one of them.

Not pictured: Kay Wegner. Photo by Tilton

Today my shop has moved from its original location to a 3800 square foot building. The classroom is about 300 square feet, and houses a Gammill quilting machine to quilt customers' quilts. I pride myself on having more samples in my store than any quilt shop around. It is touted locally as an "Art Gallery!" I teach many classes in my shop, and the revenue from my classes will always stay with my shop. It was something that I decided early on in the business. It is a way for me to buy "extras", or things that I might not normally stock.

One of the most rewarding series of classes that I offer is the year round sampler class. These classes are free, and offered the last Monday of every month. The students sign up, come to class and see a demo of the block for that month. Each month I offer a new technique, such as hand appliqué, buttonhole stitch by machine, paper piecing, or corner square triangles. The students are required to buy the supplies for that month's block. All the blocks are different sizes, and at the end of the year we get together for three days and I teach them how to sew all the blocks into one quilt. By the end of the year, a beginner student has learned just about every quilting technique, and has pieced a quilt together with all different sized blocks. No two quilts are ever alike! Then during January of the next year, we have a big quilt show for the public where all the quilts can be seen. This spurs interest for new students to sign up for the next year.

View from the balcony. Photo by Tilton

Laura's quilt, 2001, 80.5" x 80.5", Photo by Tilton

Old World Santas will be my sampler for 2002. This quilt was a combined effort with my friend Dione Roberts. Dione designed the Santas a few years ago and made them for her stained glass shop. They were great designs and I thought they would make a wonderful quilt. We needed other filler blocks to complete the quilt, so I designed those. The blocks come in 12 different patterns and can also be made into small individual wall hangings. We each pieced together our own quilt and I machine quilted both of them. We started designing the patterns in January and our quilts were completed in May. We spent a lot of time together working on them and had a great time in the process!

pieced by Dione Roberts, 2001, Photo by Tilton

Western Wear, flannel, 1996, 61" x 82"

Rag Flag, 2000, 58" x 108"

Western Wear, batik, 2001, 54" x 75"

fiberworks

After I opened the shop in 1994, **Western Wear** was the first original pattern that I designed. It was a great pattern for tourists to take home a little bit of Montana! I made the sample in flannels, and embellished it with painted star buttons. Recently I remade the quilt in batiks and updated the pattern cover. Quite a contrast from the first! It was embellished with different colored porcelain star buttons.

Rag Flag is a pattern that came from the popular "rag" technique and my love for flag quilts. This quilt is made of all red, white, and blue plaids with the seams on the outside and washed for that frayed "rag" look.

X's & O's Purple, 2001, 72.5" x 92.5", quilted by Janet Caudill

X's & O's Hugs and Kisses was a quilt that I designed for my pattern line from an inspirational bolt of batik fabric that is used for the border. Raw edge appliqué and no template piecing make this a fun quilt to make. Janet and Matt Caudill purchased the purple and teal X's and O's quilt.

X's & O's Brown, 2001, 72.5" x 92.5"

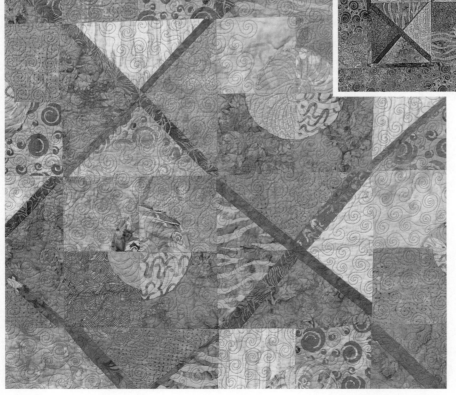

quilted by Laura Heine

Today, I am able to leave my shop more and feel comfortable. I have a great staff, who are very supportive and helpful. Without them I would not be as successful. It is very rewarding to be able to help people do what they enjoy. I am very lucky to have a job and a career that enables me to do what I love. I have met many wonderful women, and feel that I have friends all over, as quilting just creates that bond.

Ravissant, color, 2001, Photo by Tilton

fabric design

From thought to cloth...
fabric design

Designing a fabric line happened much earlier than I had anticipated. It began in 1998 with my relationship with the fabric company Kings Road Imports. Kings Road entered the quilting market in 1993 as the American distributor of an English line of cotton prints. To expand their offering in 1996, they introduced their own line of quilting fabrics.

In 1997, they invited four shop owners to help determine their next fabric line by coloring a design selected from the Kings Road Imports' design library. When I was asked to be a part of this challenge, I had a hard time choosing one of their designs to color and really wanted to do a design of my own. They were excited about the idea of an original design and I proceeded.

My design was my simple machine quilting leaf overlaid on a hand-dyed looking background, which I did in five different colorways. The challenge was that whichever of the four designers' fabrics sold the most yardage at Fall Quilt Market won. Sales of that design were so successful that they decided to print the fabric without the leaf overlay also. I had won the challenge, which enabled me to design another line with Kings Road.

I had made a verbal agreement with another company for first rights on designing my first complete line of fabrics years before, so I was in a bind. I told Kings Road about this agreement, and I submitted my new designs to the other company. It turned out that they were not interested in a style that was too different from theirs.

Pat Smith, Vice President of Kings Road, was delighted to hear the good news and wanted my designs as soon as possible to try to have them ready for Fall Quilt Market.

The name of my first line was **Fondly Flowers**. My paintings were reproduced exactly as I had painted them and it was exciting for me to see. It was new and vibrant for the time and it sold very well. The design was printed in six different colorways originally, but later reduced to four. To go along with the fabrics, I designed a free pattern for the shops that purchased them.

Kings Road Imports and YLI Corporation got together and sponsored a challenge using my fabrics and YLI threads. The quilts hung at Fall Quilt Market 2000 and was a wonderfully beautiful display of color! The winning quilts traveled on a shop tour for the following year.

2000, 67" x 98", quilted by Vi Russell

quilted by Vi Russell

Painted Petal, 2000, 72" x 82"

Painted Petal, 2001, 72" x 82".
Photo by Tilton

My next line of fabrics, **Painted Petal,** was introduced at Spring Quilt Market in 2000. The focus print was a huge flower, which was designed so that it could be used as a backing fabric. It follows the pattern of the flowers and leaves for the quilting design. It was in much lighter colors for me, very different from the previous collection.

Of course, I had to design a pattern to go along with this collection as well. It had machine embroidery, paper piecing, and a lot of machine quilting. It also had each print in the entire collection represented, in every colorway! The collection sold well, and was printed again in three new colorways, darker jewel tones, for the Fall Quilt Market.

From thought to cloth...fabric design

Pat Smith would always say that I was good at concept. I usually just agreed with her until one day I asked her what she meant by that. She said she meant that I was good at coming up with an idea of something, formed by combining all its characteristics, then constructing a project to take the collection to another level. I could take fabric and see how it could be used. I had not realized this until she said it. When I would design something, in the back of my mind I was always nervous because I knew that I would need to prove that something could be made from what I was doing and I tried not to let this hinder me when I was designing.

When we decided to run the *Painted Petal* collection again, Pat asked me for another free pattern. She said, "We need something that showcases the line of fabrics, and is easy, and will make the customer want to buy the line of fabrics." No pressure at all, right? The only idea that I could come up with was my original idea of quilting from the back of the quilt, using the large primary floral as the quilting design.

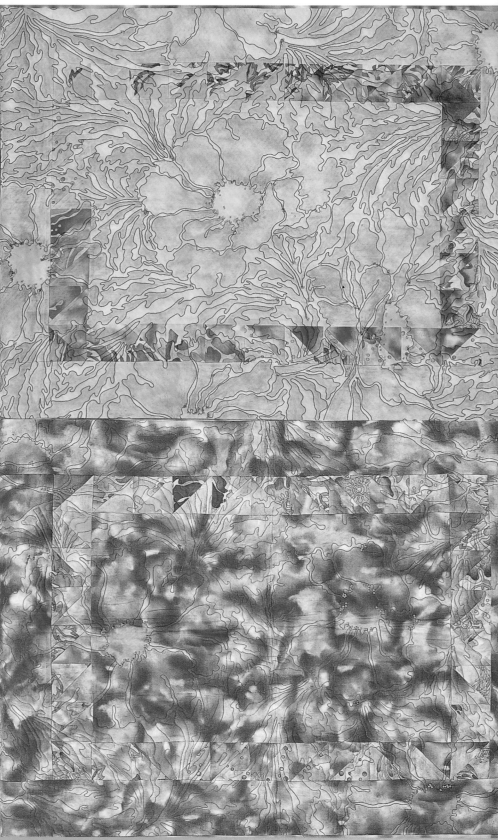

Quilted Petal, 2000, 22" x 28"

I pieced a triangle border with the other prints in the collection, used the solid from that colorway, put the large print on the back and quilted it upside down with contrasting threads. I got out my box of 96 crayons and did some shading around the flower petals and leaves on the solid. Then I sent the quilt off to Kings Road. I thought it was a great "concept".

I didn't hear from Pat for a few days, and began to wonder if she received the quilt. I called her and she said she had. I was all excited, and asked her if she liked it. She said it was "OK", but that it didn't really showcase my fabrics.

Off they went to a market in Las Vegas. She called me on the phone several times from there to tell me how great the fabric was doing...the little quilt was doing it's job. "You would not believe it!," she kept saying. I just said "Really!"

Quilted Petal (back)

Color Fusion

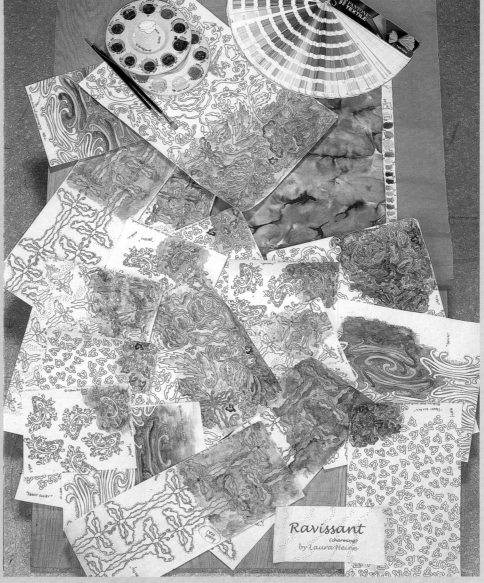

Photo by Tilton

Let me take you through the whole process of creating a line of quilt fabrics using my newest collection called *Ravissant*.

First I look for inspiration to give me an idea for a theme. I look at flowers, nature, books... everywhere. Then I draw it out on paper. This process can be the most time-consuming because it takes me a long time to draw.

Many times I will use the copier to enlarge or reduce the design to get just the perfect size.

After deciding on the main design, I need to design coordinates to make a collection. Sometimes these can be small motifs of the original design. For example, in the Ravissant collection I pulled out the center heart shape of the rose flower for a tossed heart pattern.

opposite page, Ravissant black and white. Photo by Tilton

From thought to cloth... design process

Color is next. I don't need to paint the entire collection, only a portion of it, so that I can be sure that I like the color combinations, and to be sure that the artists of Kings Road understand what I want. When I send it all to Kings Road for approval, they have their artists actually paint it and determine the fabric repeat. Then it comes back to me.

Kings Road screen prints their fabrics in Japan where each screen represents one color. When I choose my colors I need to stay within their maximum of fifteen different colors in each colorway. Sometimes this is very hard to do.

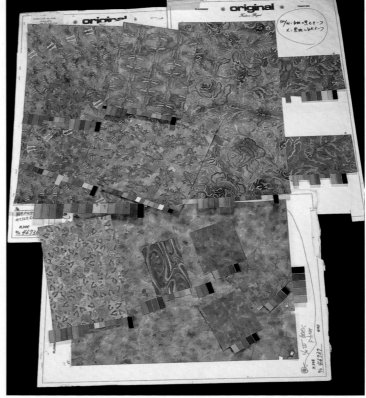

Original paintings from Japan. Photo by Tilton

The final painted designs are sent to Japan for strike-offs. Strike-off is the term applied to the first few yards that come off the printing machine. They are used for the purpose of evaluation. I review the strike-offs and determine if any changes or corrections need to be made, and if so, they are made at this time. After final approval, the fabric is then printed.

When I design a fabric, I can't think of all of this at once. I only take one step at a time. If I don't limit myself, I will draw a blank. Each collection has become easier to do, because I have a process now. When I started, I wasn't exactly sure what the company needed, and how I would communicate what I wanted to them.

Strike-offs. Photo by Tilton

Now, our relationship has developed into a great partnership. Pat and I collaborated on two new collections, **Duet**, which was introduced at Spring Quilt Market in 2001. It gave us an opportunity to develop two more collections that could integrate designs from two very different designers, combining both our senses of style and color.

I really couldn't believe all this was happening. When the first line of fabrics came, I just looked at it. It was hard to believe that what I drew was on fabric. When the second line came, I cried. When the third line came I cried again! One day soon after the *Painted Petal* fabric came to the shop, I was working in the store on a very busy day. I looked around and almost every customer in the store had a *Painted Petal* fabric bolt in their hands. It was such a great feeling.

We all wonder whether people will "come to the party;" well I wondered if anyone would "buy the fabric." Sometimes today I still look at the fabric and it doesn't seem real that I did them. I truly feel that there is a higher being out there guiding me as I create.

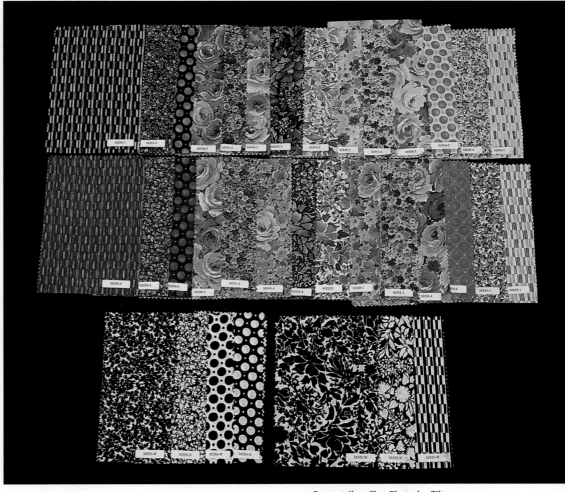

Duet strike-offs. Photo by Tilton

Painted Petal fabrics in warehouse.

Drawing with the machine needle

pieced by John Flynn, 1989, 49" x 76"

When I started quilting fifteen years ago, I hand quilted all of my tops. I just felt that you were cheating if you machine quilted. If I chose to have a quilt machine quilted, I sent it out and that quilt then lived on a bed. It just wasn't the same as a hand quilted one and none of my "precious" quilts were ever machine quilted.

Very quickly my tops began to create a pile that encompassed a large closet space. Tops are just what they were and how they stayed. I would never get them all hand quilted if I continued to piece at this pace. Finally, I decided to take a machine quilting class from a friend, Kristy Osborne, who did wonderful machine quilting. She encouraged me to start doing it too. So, off to the class I went, with one of those "not-so-cherished" quilt tops. I decided that I would hold to my philosophy that hand quilting would never be replaced in my heart, and that I would just learn how to machine quilt so I could get some of these tops finished.

opposite page:
Flower Baskets, 2001, 64" x 91.5",
Photo by Tilton.

Drawing with the machine needle

As it turned out, I had the time of my life. I started free-motion stippling with fairly small stippling. I had more control that way, and could get better-rounded edges. We didn't have the threads to choose from back then, so I started out machine quilting with metallic threads. My first machine quilted piece was a top that was pieced for me by John Flynn, an international quilting instructor and artist. It was a guild "brown bag" and John drew my name. How lucky was I!

A "brown bag" is just that, a bag with someone else's fabric in it. The bags were distributed randomly, and you never knew who got your bag until the end. I had put fabric in my bag that matched my couch at the time, so I knew that this would be a usable quilt. Once I got the hand-foot coordination of free-motion quilting down, it was fun and quite relaxing for me.

I decided after that first quilt that maybe I needed to change my thinking about machine quilting. So I started sneaking in a machine-quilted quilt once in awhile, and before I knew it, I didn't even remember how to hand quilt. I have been machine quilting now for 12 years, and continue to learn new things every day.

Machine Basics

Many times I am asked, "Which machine do you prefer to use?" or "what machine do you quilt with?" I do have my preferences, but I tend to get in trouble giving out my opinion. So what I say is, you need to "test drive" the machines on your own. You should bring in the thread that you want to quilt with and be sure the machine can sew with it before you purchase it.

There are a few features though that I could not live without:
1. Feed dogs must be able to be lowered.
2. Buttonhole stitch is a great feature that is used often by quilters.
3. Bobbin case that comes out and can be adjusted easily.
4. Needle down feature.

Basic Tools

Batting
Polyester vs. Cotton? Polyester battings are very lightweight, inexpensive and easier to care for, but they are not considered "breathable". They are more sensitive to heat, and tend to build up body heat when used in quilts for beds. They also have a tendency to "beard" or pull through to the quilt top when quilted. The fibers migrate through to the fabric layers. Cotton battings "breathe" and tend to be warm in cool weather and cool in hot weather. Cotton battings are much better than they were years ago, due to a process called "needle punching". Needle punching breaks up the density of the cotton fiber during the manufacturing process, which allows for easier quilting. Cotton batting comes natural/unbleached or pure white/bleached. This is important when light background fabrics are chosen for a project. There are also cotton-poly blend battings available. The polyester is usually 20% and provides somewhat of a stabilizer to the cotton fibers, and it also allows you to quilt at larger intervals.

Binder Clips

Binder clips can be purchased at an office supply store. You need the largest clips, 1" capacity. They are used to stretch the backing fabric to a table in preparation for pin basting the quilt. You will need a maximum of one box of 12 for any size quilt.

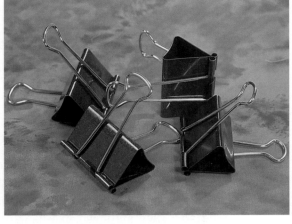

binder clips

Darning or Quilting Foot

The darning foot was originally designed for mending. There are many shapes of darning feet, and it is important to have the correct foot for your machine. The foot allows free movement of the fabric as you stitch. The feed dogs are lowered or covered and the foot rests lightly on the fabric when the needle enters the fabric. The darning foot is used for all free motion quilting.

darning or quilting foot

Walking Foot

The walking foot, or even-feed foot, is an attachment that you must buy to fit your individual machine. It is a foot that has feed dogs that will move with the lower feed dogs of your machine so that all the layers of the fabric move together. You must use a walking foot whenever you do straight line quilting. It will help prevent tucks on the front and back of the quilt.

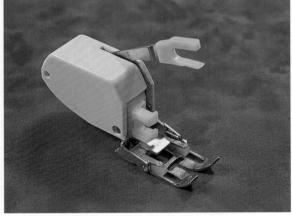

walking foot

Marking tools

I very seldom mark my quilting lines but when I do, I prefer the Anita's Graphite Pencil for lighter fabrics, or the Anita's Soapstone pencil for dark fabrics. These pencils are completely washable. But there are many other types of marking tools that work well.

marking tool

Drawing with the machine needle

Quilter's Gloves

Quilter's gloves are gloves with small round plastic adhesives attached to them for ease in gripping and maneuvering the fabric while quilting. They are much like garden gloves. I prefer the cotton gloves and I cut the fingers off of each hand so threads do not stick to them.

gloves

Safety Pins & Pin Closing Tool

I use 1″ long nickel-plated safety pins. The nickel plating prevents rusting of the pin. You will need about 10 gross for a queen size quilt, pinning every 1-1/2″ to 2″ apart. I use a pin closing tool called the Kwick Klip. It holds the pin tip up so the head can close over it with ease.

Needles

Refer to the needle suggestions on the Threads chart. Most often I use the 90/14 machine embroidery needle for all threads for machine quilting. I have found that this needle tolerates most of the threads that I use. It is important to change your needle often, as it becomes dull and will cause the thread to break or shred.

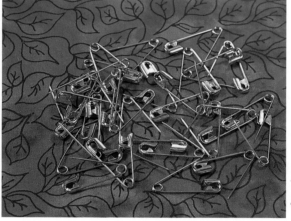
safety pins

closing tool

opposite page, Kaleidoscope Krazy

Drawing with the machine needle

Threads I Love

Sample	Thread	Weight	Colors	Needle Size	Uses
	YLI Colours Variegated 100% long staple cotton	30, 3 ply	Primaries, violets, reds, light blues, dark blues, greens	80/12 sharp or 90/14 embroidery	Great decorative thread for machine quilting and embroidery. Can be used through the needle, in the bobbin, or both.
	YLI Machine Quilting Thread Extra long staple Peruvian cotton	40, 3 ply	6 solid colors and 12 variegated combinations	80/12 sharp or 90/14 for regular machines, 3.5-4.0 for long arm machines	Great quality thread for long arm quilting as well as regular quilting. Can be used through the needle, in the bobbin, or both.
	YLI Wonder Invisible monofilament	.04	Smoke for dark fabrics and clear for light fabrics	90/14-machine embroidery	Used in machine quilting for the "hand quilted" look, or when the thread color would detract from the pieced quilt.
	YLI Quilting Thread 100% long staple cotton	40, 3 ply	24 different solid colors	90/14 machine embroidery needle	For machine and hand quilting. Glazed with a starch versus a wax. Can be used through the needle, in the bobbin, or both.
	YLI Fine Metallic	40	23 different colors, including variegated	90/14-machine embroidery needle	Quilts just a glimmer of a shine. Can be used through the needle, or in the bobbin.

Threads I Love

Sample	Thread	Weight	Colors	Needle Size	Uses
	YLI Ultrasheen Acrylic	40	50 colors including variegated	90/14- machine embroidery or 75/11 machine embroidery	Works well for machine embroidery. Has a "transparent" quality that will let the thread below show through if you are stacking up threads. Use for machine quilting either through the needle, in the bobbin, or both.
	YLI Jeans Stitch	30, 3 ply	24 solid colors and 4 variegated colors	90/14- machine embroidery or 100 Jeans denim needle	Top stitch thread. 100% poly-ester. Great thread for machine quilting, will give a heavy decorative thread line. Can be used either through the needle or in the bobbin, but I don't recommend using it for both.
	YLI Select	40, 2 ply	24 solid colors	80/12 sharp or 90/14- machine embroidery	This is an all-purpose version of the Quilting Thread. It is excellent for piecing, appliqué and all-purpose sewing. Can be used for quilting through the needle, in the bobbin, or both.
	YLI Glow Bug*	25, 210d/2	1	110 Topstitch needle	Exciting luminous thread! Sensitive to heat, do not dry clean or place in the dryer. It is charged when it is exposed to any light source. Great for machine embroidery or quilting. Can be used through the needle, or in the bobbin, but not both.
	Oliver Twist cotton	50	many different variegated combinations	80/12 sharp	Hand dyed embroidery weight thread from England. A great thread for machine embellishing and embroidery. May be too fine to quilt with, but it can be run through the needle, in the bobbin or both.

*quilted by Sandi Carr

Drawing with the machine needle

Threads I Love

Sample	Thread	Weight	Colors	Needle Size	Uses
	Sulky Rayon	30 or 40	Hundreds of solids and dozens of variegated combinations	80/12 sharp or 90/14 machine embroidery	Decorative rayon, good for machine embroidery and/or embellishing. Can be used for quilting, through the needle, in the bobbin, or both.
	YLI Reflections*	40	10 different shades	90/14 machine embroidery	This is truly a thread of a different color! The actual color of the thread will vary depending on the fabric, the light source, as well as other environmental influences. Because of the unique manufacturing process the color can also vary from dye lot to dye lot. Can be used through the needle or in the bobbin.
	Signature 100% cotton thread	40wt 3 ply	36 solids and 7 variegated color combinations	80/12 Universal or 90/14 Machine Embroidery	Great for long arm quilting machines and regular sewing machines for machine quilting.
	YLI Wash Away Thread			75/11 Embroidery or 80/12 Universal	This wash away basting thread is used for securing the batting to the back of the quilt top during machine trapunto. Once the quilt has been quilted, the basting thread will wash away, leaving just the trapunto work. Some quilters prefer to use this thread for basting the layers of the quilt top together before machine or hand quilting.

*quilted by Sandi Carr

Pin Basting the Quilt

I have outlined a few of the basics for machine quilting that I feel are important. These are the steps that people tend NOT to do, or skimp on. In my experience, they will make or break your quilt.

1. Start by squaring up your quilt top. If your quilt top is not square after it is pieced, it won't be square after it is quilted.

2. Be sure the backing fabric and batting are at least 4" larger than the quilt around all four sides.

3. Stretch the backing fabric of the quilt, wrong side up to a table, with 1" capacity binder clips. If you can't clip all four edges, use a heavy duty packaging tape to secure the unclipped edges of the quilt.

4. Lay the batting on the quilt backing. Be sure there are no tucks or puckers in the batting.

5. Lay the quilt top over the batting, right side up, smoothing from the center out.

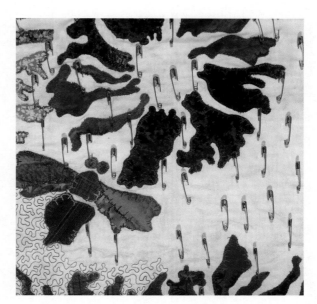

6. Use #1 nickel-plated safety pins, and pin the quilt every 1-1/2" to 2" apart. Start pinning from the center of the quilt and work out to the edges.

Now you are ready to quilt!

It is important to start quilting from the center of your quilt working out. That way, if you do have any extra fullness it will be worked to the outer edges. Remove the safety pins from your quilt as they come up to the machine table. You need to have a large area to work so you will not run over pins. As you take your pins out, put them in a metal tin, leaving them open so they will be ready to baste the next quilt.

Relax and try not to get all tensed up! Remember the faster you go with your foot the more control you will have. When you first begin quilting, don't worry about stacking your stitches. Go fast with your foot, and focus more on curved lines. Your stitch length will come with time and practice.

Drawing with the machine needle

Helpful Hints

1. Use a "pin closer" when you are pin basting your quilt. Once you learn how to use it, it will save your fingers and time!

2. Always quilt with a clean, oiled machine. A machine cannot sew properly if it is dirty and needs oiling. Check your owner's manual for how often to oil.

3. If your thread is breaking for no apparent reason, or is getting wound around the spool holder, put the spool of thread in a small jar behind the machine and then thread as usual.

4. When starting to quilt, pull the bobbin thread up to the top of the quilt before you begin to machine quilt. This will prevent bobbin tails that will need to be trimmed from the bottom.

5. Use high-quality sewing machine needles and change your needle often. Needles are the least expensive items you use for quilting and the most important! They quickly become dull or can acquire a burr, which will cause the thread to break or shred. In general use a 90/14 machine embroidery needle for almost all decorative threads. This will also work for the heavier YLI Jeans Stitch thread. If your thread is breaking at the site of the needle, the needle is not large enough. With batiks, or very tightly woven fabrics, you may need to go up to a size 100 needle. Be careful using a 100 needle, it can leave holes in some fabrics. Test first on a scrap.

6. Try using different threads on the same quilt. They will add more interest and texture to the quilt.

7. Try to limit your marking of the quilt. Teach yourself to draw the design from your mind. It will be difficult at first, but with practice it will come. You will end up saving more time and be more creative if it comes out of your head! When I see a new design that I want to try, I start by drawing it with a pencil on paper. Then I practice on the machine and scrap fabric.

8. Quilt consistently over the entire surface of the quilt. Don't quilt small and tightly, in one area and then looser and larger in others. That would cause your quilt to ripple. You can change designs within the same quilt, but keep the size of the design consistent.

9. Use backing fabrics with great quilting designs and quilt your quilt from the back with the bobbin work technique (page 91). This works especially well when you don't know how else to quilt it! If you choose to do this, you must treat your backing as the quilt top. The pins will be on the backing fabric. You must pay very close attention to the bobbintension, as the bobbin thread will be on the top of your quilt.

10. Know your batting and its quilting requirements. You must follow the manu-facturer's recommendations on quilting distance. Cotton requires anywhere from 1" apart to 10" apart depending on how it was manufactured.

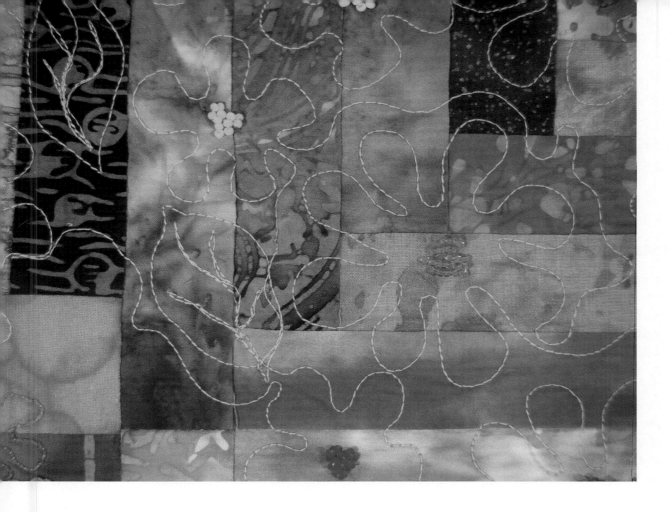

Somewhat Off Center (detail)

Bobbin Quilting

When I was ready to quilt *Somewhat off Center*, the log cabin quilt that was pieced with contemporary colors, I was at a loss as to how it should be quilted. I had an idea that I could quilt upside down, using the backing fabric as my quilting pattern. I found a great batik fabric with little flowers on it which I pinned as the top. I stretched the pieced top on the table upside down, added the batting then the backing and the pins went into this backing fabric. In the bobbin I used the thick variegated Jeans Stitch thread, and cotton through the needle.

It is important to keep an eye on the bobbin tension during the quilting. The bobbin thread will be showing on the top of the quilt, so the tension in the bobbin must be balanced. You can use different threads in the bobbin and through the needle, just practice first to get balanced tension before starting on your quilt.

Look for fabrics with outline designs, or easy motifs to trace with the machine needle. Overlapping flowers and leaves can be difficult to do and confusing to the eye on the quilt top.

good fabrics to follow for quilting

Drawing with the machine needle

Innovative Machine Quilting Designs

These are free motion quilting designs that I use frequently. The quilting design is an important element of the quilt and should be chosen with care. Once you have chosen a design, practice it, and reduce or enlarge it to fit your quilt or block. Remember, your quilting will be your handwriting, and not necessarily look exactly like mine. As you play with my designs, I am sure that you will come up with ones of your own. Make a notebook of designs, as you will forget them if you don't! Have fun, and remember to think of your machine needle as the pencil!

Designs shown have been reduced 50%.

connected triangle

daisy

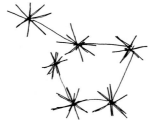

dandelions

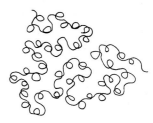

loopdeloops

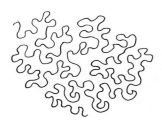

basic stipple

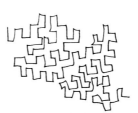

square stipple

folky flowers

snails

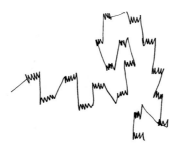

zip connected to zag

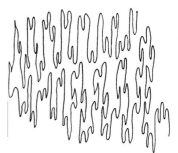

seaweed tree bark water

Laura's leaf vine

whirlygig

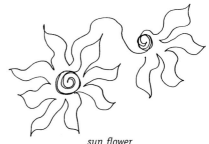

sun flower

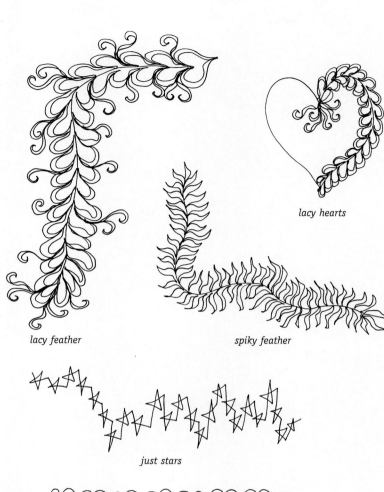

lacy feather　　*spiky feather*

lacy hearts

just for fun

vertical hearts

heartlike leaves

just stars

ocean waves

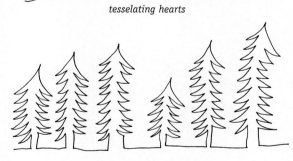

tesselating hearts

basically bad EKG

folky trees

loops & stars

horizontal hearts

Laura Laura Laura Laura

your name

tulips

pineapple top border

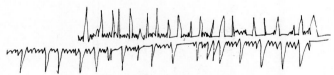

grass

Flowers and Flies, 1998, 56.5" x 79"

Free motion embroidery
and embellishing

I wasn't machine quilting for long before I realized that there was an entire world of thread out there. It started with the use of wonderfully different threads for machine quilting, which led to using threads for machine embellishing. I found myself stitching thread on the quilt tops before I quilted them. It added dimension and texture and a completely new design element, some of which totally changed the look of the quilt. I don't really know how this whole process came about. Maybe I needed to secure edges of a fused quilt, and it took off from there.

When I first started machine embroidery and embellishing, I would keep track of the amounts of thread that I used on a quilt. Some of my quilts have the thread yardage written on the quilt labels. I stopped doing that once I opened the shop. I overheard a customer say, "That isn't quilting. It is an internal struggle with her to see how much thread she can put on a quilt." Maybe so, but I love it.

Basic tools for machine embroidery

8-10" machine embroidery hoop
90/14 machine embroidery needles
Threads...lots of them!
Fused quilt top
Darning foot for your machine

Basics of fusible appliqué

Choose a fusible material that is appropriate to the pattern you are using. I prefer Steam-a-Seam 2 because of its double stick quality. It can be moved around on the background many times, and will stick before the final fuse is done, enabling you to get all your motifs in their proper position on the quilt top before making the final fuse. There are several types of fusibles on the market that you can try.

Free motion embroidery and embellishing

1. Trace the motifs to the paper side of the fusible. If using Steam-A-Seam 2, draw your pattern to the paper side that sticks the best.

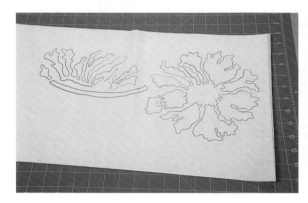

2. Rough cut around the drawn motif.

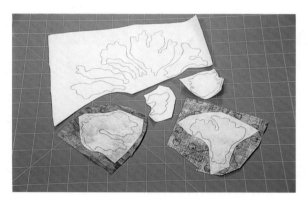

3. Remove the backing paper of the fusible and fuse it to the wrong side of the appliqué fabric.

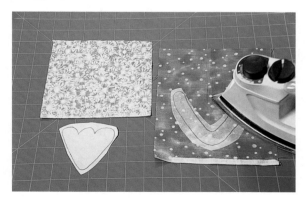

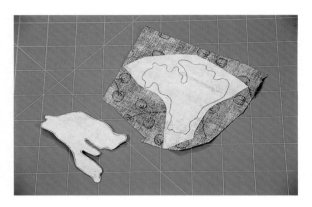

4. Cut out the motif on the lines.

5. Place the motif in the proper position on the quilt top.

6. Make the final fuse after all motifs are on the quilt top in their correct position.

7. Place an 8-10" wooden embroidery hoop on the fused quilt top, with the screw closure on the bottom of the quilt, so that it will sit flush with the sewing machine deck. Tighten the hoop so the quilt top is as tight as a drum.

8. The fused motifs will need to be embroidered down to secure the edges. This can be done with a free motion straight stitch, or zig zag stitch.

Machine Embellishing

Basics of Trapunto

Machine trapunto can be started once the machine embroidery is completed. You will need a wash-away basting thread in the needle, and a cotton thread for the bobbin.

1. Place a thin layer of cotton batting behind the area you wish to trapunto. Make it a bit larger all around than the area you wish to stitch and pin on the top.

2. With the wash-away thread through the needle, free-motion stitch around the motif. Turn the quilt over and cut away any extra batting beyond the stitching line.

3. Once the machine trapunto is finished, the quilt is layered with the batting and backing fabric and quilted everywhere except within the trapunto area. Keep in mind the quilting needs to be fairly small for the trapunto to "puff" out. Stitch right up to the edge of the trapunto work.

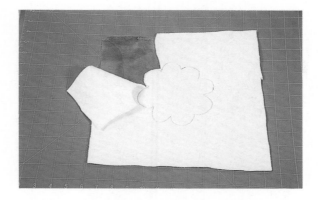

4. Once the quilting is done, if the trapunto area is quite large, you can outline inner motifs such as the flowers in "Floret" to give additional interest to your trapunto. You can also add lines of thread for interest such as stamens for flowers. By adding inner lines to the trapunto, it seems to secure the trapunto and, at the same time, adds another dimension.

5. When the quilt is finished, washing the quilt, or spraying it with water will remove the "wash-away" thread. The bobbin thread from the trapunto work will remain within the layers of the quilt.

Bead and Button Embellishments

I started using buttons and beads for embellishments when I made the *Field Of Flowers* quilt in 1995. I felt that the flowers just needed some additional interest, and the beads and buttons provided that. I collected many colorful, different buttons and beads for the quilt, and hand stitched them to the centers of the flowers. It added so much interest, and I watch people touch and study the buttons on that quilt now!

Buttons can be sewn on so that they appear to have a bicycle tire look, meaning the thread comes out of the center of the hole of the button and goes across to the side of the button and then down into the quilt forming "spokes".

They can also be sewn randomly on the quilt just for a decorative look.

Beading can be fun to do in the centers of flowers, so the flower appears to have pollen in them.

Glow Bug has a lot of different beading done in the plain center squares and then iridescent beads for eyes of the bugs. It was fun to see how much the quilt changed with adding the bead embellishments.

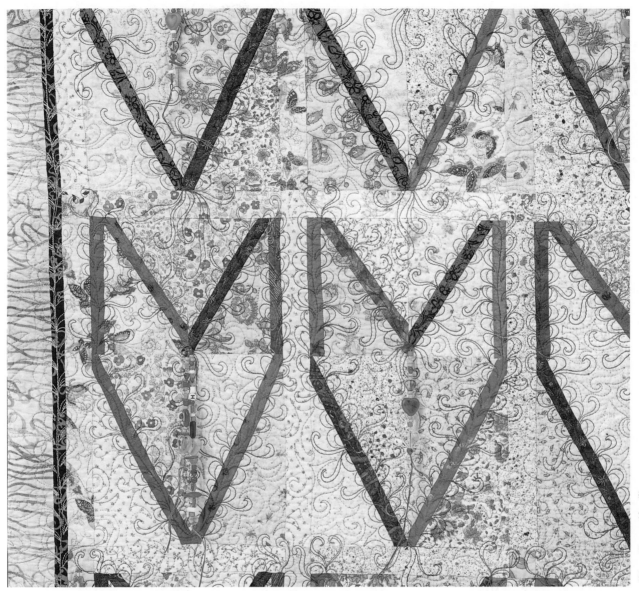

After completing the *Skinny Hearts* quilt, and a recent visit to a wonderful bead shop in Ohio, I decided to sew strands of beads in the centers of some of the hearts. Most of the beads are red, pink and white and are in heart shapes, following the theme of the quilt. It was fun to see just how many heart buttons I could find. One of the hearts has a brass "hand" button sewn to the center of the heart, and inside of the hand I placed a tiny heart. Once I started, the ideas just seemed to flow.

There was a time when sewing beads on by sewing machine was a trend. I did sew many beads on in this manner, but have found that I enjoy sewing them on by hand much more. I find that it is not really any faster to sew them on by machine, and they tend to be more secure by hand.

Embellishments on your quilts will add so much more interest, and you will find that it is quite fun! Start collecting interesting buttons and beads. Add them to your fabric stash, and the right quilt will come one day that "calls" for these embellishments.

Jane'squilt

Finished size: 45" wide x 31" long
Patterns page 135
Triangles pattern page 136

supplies

- 1-1/3 yards of background and outer border fabric (same fabric)

- 1/4 yard of 6 different red to purple fabrics for triangle border, flowers and bugs

- 1/4 yard of 4 different green fabrics for triangle border, leaves and stems

- 1-1/2 yards of backing fabric

- YLI variegated Colours thread in red variegated and green variegated for machine embroidery

- Neutral color cotton thread for the bobbin for machine embroidery

- 90/14 machine embroidery needles

- 8" wooden machine embroidery hoop

- 2 yards of Steam-a-Seam 2 fusible

- Appliqué pressing sheet

- Thread of choice for machine quilting

- 1 yard of light weight cotton batting

- Optional: 2" finished Half Square Triangles-on-a-Roll

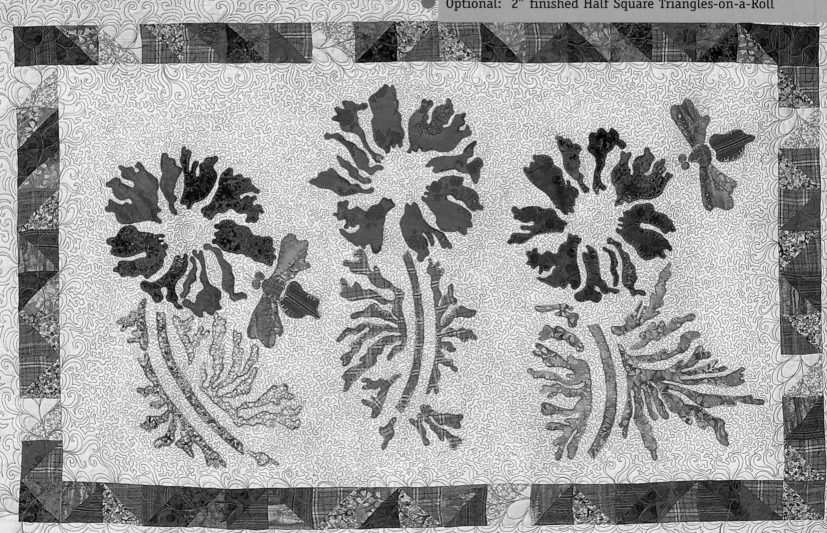

Jane Ohnstad is a great customer of mine. We got to know each other when she came into the shop frequently and took many classes. She knew that I collected yo-yo quilts so when she found an antique yo-yo quilt at a garage sale, she bought it for me. She doesn't like yo-yo quilts while I love them, maybe because I can appreciate all the time-consuming work that goes into them. I have about 10 different yo-yo quilts in my collection, mostly antiques.

Anyway, Jane bought this quilt for $10. How would you feel if you were the lady who spent her life making this quilt?! She brought it into the shop and tempted me with it! The deal she proposed was that I make her a quilt, using all my thread techniques, and it could be mine!

Well, how could you refuse an offer like that? Besides, I wanted that poor $10 quilt to have some value and a good home! So here is the quilt that I made for Jane. She had a spot in her house that measured 50" wide by 40" tall that she wanted me to fill. Oh, the challenge of commissions!

Antique yo-yo quilt

1. Cut the center fabric 20–1/2" x 34-1/2"

2. Make 8 photocopies of the triangle grid. I prefer to use the 2" finished triangles on a roll. I have found many photo copy machines alter the size of the copy, making the pieced triangles off slightly.

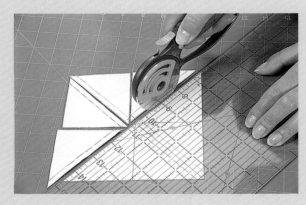

3. Cut 16 (6-1/2") squares from the triangle border fabrics. You will need to cut 2 each of a few to yield 16 squares since you have a total of 10 triangle border fabrics. Make 8 sets with different fabrics in each set, and put their right sides together.

4. Place the grid paper over the top of the fabric sets and sew on the dotted lines of the paper. Cut the triangles apart on the solid lines, remove the paper and press. You will only need 58 of these half square triangle squares.

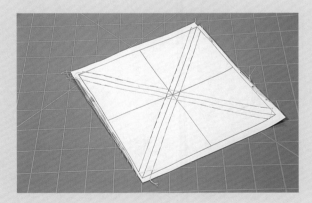

Jane'squilt

5. Sew together two rows of 10 half square triangles for the sides.

6. Sew one row to each side of the center piece. Press seams toward the border if you have a light fabric, otherwise press seam towards the center.

7. Sew together two rows of 19 half-square triangles for the top and bottom.

8. Sew one set to the top of the quilt and one to the bottom. Press seams toward the border if you have a light fabric, otherwise press the seam toward the center.

9. Cut 2 (24-1/2" x 4") outer border strips and sew them to each side of the quilt. Press seams.

10. Cut and piece 2 (45-1/2" x 4") outer border strips and sew them to the top and bottom of the quilt. Press seams.

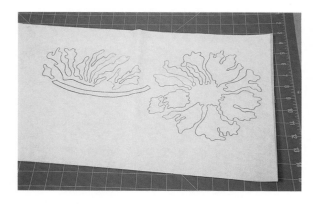

11. Trace the flowers, leaves and bugs to Steam-a-Seam 2 fusible.

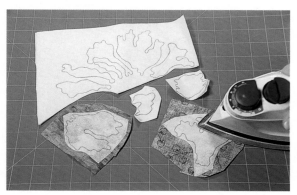

12. Rough cut around the fusible, remove the backing paper and fuse it to the wrong side of each corresponding fabric. Use an appliqué pressing sheet to protect your iron and ironing board.

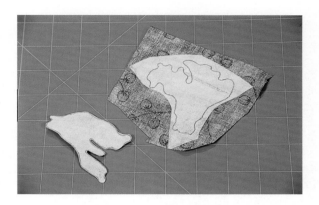

13. Cut the design on the line, and place it in its approximate location on the quilt top. Continue with each pattern until all the pieces are placed on the quilt top.

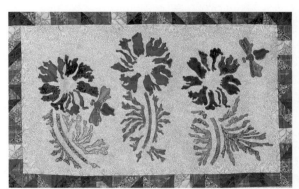

14. Once you have all your pieces in the desired position, fuse them to the quilt.

15. Set your machine up for free motion work. Your feed dogs should be down and the darning foot on. Put the neutral cotton thread in the bobbin, and the YLI Colours thread for embroidery through the needle.

16. Place the fused section of the quilt to be embroidered in the machine embroidery hoop with the screw closure on the wrong side of the quilt top. The hoop will lay flush with the sewing machine table.

17. Your machine should be set on straight stitching. Moving your hoop in small back and forth movements, create a free motion satin stitch. Make the length of the stitching lines uneven for an added decorative look. Begin at the edge of each fused piece, and work completely around that section. Complete each fused shape with this technique, changing threads on the leaves and bug parts.

18. Prepare the quilt for machine quilting.

Machine Quilting

Refer to Drawing With the Machine Needle for designs for quilting.

floret**quilt**

Finished size: 40" x 40"
Patterns page 136

- 3/4 yard of center background fabric
- 1/2 yard of inner border fabric
- 1/2 yard of focus floral fabric for outer border
- 1/4 yard each of 5-6 different solids for flowers and flower centers
- 1/2 yard each of 2 different green fabrics for stems and leaves
- 1-1/2 yards of fabric for backing
- 1/2 yard of fabric for binding
- Heavy embellishing yarn or thread
- YLI Monofilament thread for couching
- YLI Jeans Stitch threads for machine embroidery in a variety of colors

- cotton thread for bobbin
- 3 yards of Steam-A-Seam 2
- 1-1/2 yards of lightweight cotton batting for trapunto and machine quilting. Cut into two 40 x 40 pieces.
- YLI variegated cotton thread for decorative quilting
- beads for embellishing
- appliqué pressing sheet
- 8" wooden machine embroidery hoop
- YLI Wash-Away thread for machine trapunto

1. Cut the center background fabric and all border fabrics according to the diagram. Sew the two 3-1/2" x 24-1/2" inner borders to the top and bottom of the center square. Sew the two 3-1/2" x 30-1/2" inner border fabrics to the sides of the center square. Press all seams towards the border.

2. Sew the two 5-1/2" x 30-1/2" outer border fabrics to the top and bottom of the quilt. Piece the two 5-1/2" x 40-1/2" outer border fabrics to the sides of the quilt. Press all seams towards the borders.

		cut 5½" x 30½"		
cut 5½" x 40½"	cut 3½" x 30½"	cut 3½" x 24½"	cut 3½" x 30½"	cut 5½" x 40½"
		cut 24½" square		
		cut 3½" x 24½"		
		cut 5½" x 30½"		

floret**quilt**

3. Trace all design motifs to Steam-a-Seam 2. Each segment of the flowers need to be traced individually onto the fusible web.

4. Rough cut around each pattern on the fusible web and place the piece on the wrong side of the desired fabric. Using an appliqué pressing sheet to protect your iron and ironing board, fuse the piece to the wrong side of the fabric.

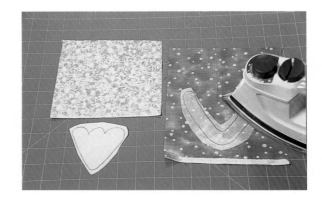

5. Cut the motifs out on the lines and place them in their proper positions on the quilt top. (see diagram) Steam-a-Seam 2 will provide "stick" at this time. Do not make the final fuse until all motifs are placed exactly as desired.

6. Using the appliqué pressing sheet, fuse the flowers and leaf/stems to the quilt top. Be sure that you have a hot iron so the pieces are securely fused to the quilt top.

Placement Guide

7. Set up your machine for free motion work. With feed dogs down and the darning foot on, put the cotton thread in the bobbin and YLI Jeans Stitch thread through the needle.

8. Place the fused section of the quilt to be embroidered in the machine embroidery hoop with the screw closure on the wrong side of the quilt top. The hoop/fabric will lay flush with the sewing machine table.

9. Program your machine with a wide zig-zag stitch and generously fill in the tulip flower sections by moving the hoop. You may find that when using the Jeans Stitch thread you may need to tighten your tension somewhat. You can even tighten it so that the bobbin thread will come up to the top of the quilt, adding another decorative touch.

   Hint: Change your threads on different fused parts of the flower, and don't try to match threads with fabric color. It will be more interesting if threads are different colors than the fabric. Stay within the fused section of the tulip flowers with the zig zag machine embroidery, but try to catch all the fused edges.

10. Change your machine to a free motion straight stitch. Stitch stamen lines from the bottom of the tulip flowers up and into the background fabric. Do this by just moving the hoop in a slow, snakelike motion. Move the hoop up the flower and into the background, then trace your line back down to the bottom of the flower and start another stamen line from the same point.

    Hint: Stamen colors can be all different too, and contrasting to the colors used in the flower.

floret**quilt**

11. With your machine on free motion straight stitching, stitch around the outer edges of the four corner and center flowers close to cut edge. Make sure that you are catching the outer fused edge of the fabric, and use contrasting thread with the fabric. Make three to four outlines around each single flower. Complete all five flowers in this way.

12. Leaving your machine set on the straight stitch and free motion, try stitching some leaves and vines in a continuous pattern on the leaf and stem fabric sections. Begin by stitching the outer edge of the leaf, coming back to your starting point, then go inside the leaf and make the veins. The leaf stitching can sneak onto the background of the quilt. When you are making the leaves, try to catch as much of the fused appliqué edge as you can. Complete all the leaf/stem sections of the quilt in this way.

13. Trapunto: Layer one 40" x 40" section of batting behind your quilt top. Pin it to the quilt top just to be sure it does not shift.

14. With the Wash-away thread in the needle of the machine, and cotton thread in the bobbin, free motion stitch around the outside of the fused appliqués. It should be one continuous line only around the OUTSIDE edges of the motifs. If your machine embroidery stitching has gone into the background, for instance in the leaf/stem section of the quilt, ignore the stitching and stay right close to the fused edge of the appliqué.

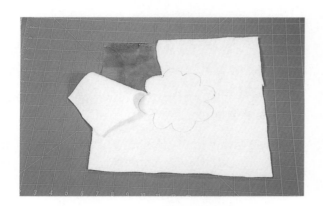

15. Using a pair of blunt tip scissors, trim away the excess batting close to the stitching line, without cutting through the stitching line or the quilt top.

16. Couching the embellishing threads/yarns: Put the monofilament thread in the needle of the machine, cotton thread in the bobbin, and change back to a free motion zig zag stitch. The zig zag will need to be wide enough to cover the embellishing thread. Lay the embellishing thread in a soft random flow down the seam connecting the inner border and center square. You can put loops in the embellishing thread too.

17. Free motion stitch with the zig zag over the embellishing thread. This is like couching, except the feed dogs are down to make it easier to deal with curves and loops. You will only need to tack this thread down, because we will machine quilt over it later. So don't stress if you don't get your zig zag exactly lined up over your embellishing thread.

Note: The embellishing threads can be couched with a regular machine foot (see photo) by having the feed dogs up and zig zagging over the thread. It is more difficult to get tight curves with this type of couching.

Machine Quilting

Refer to Drawing With the Machine Needle for ideas on quilting for the Floret quilt top.

quiltedpetal

Finished Size: 22" x 28"
Triangle pattern and guide page 136

This pattern was originally designed to be used with the "Painted Petal" fabric line that I designed for Kings Road Imports. Other fabrics can be substituted.

1 (12-1/2" x 18-1/2") rectangle of solid fabric for center

2 (3-1/2" x 16-1/2") strips of solid fabric for outer borders

2 (3-1/2" x 28-1/2") strips of solid fabric for outer borders

1 yard of a large floral fabric for the backing. It must have a good quilting design that can be followed.

1 (6-1/2") square of six coordinating print fabrics for the triangle borders

1 (6-1/2") square of six different coordinating solid fabrics for the triangle borders

26" x 32" of light-weight cotton batting

Photocopies of the triangles for paper piecing or 2" finished Triangles-on-A-Roll.

Crayons...get a big box of 96 colors!

Thread for quilting in reds for flowers and greens for leaves

Beads for embellishing

Optional:
22" x 28" frame or 1/4 yard of fabric for binding

1. Make 6 photocopies of the triangle grid for paper piecing. I prefer to use the 2" finished half square Triangles on a Roll. I have found that many photo copy machines alter the size of the copy, making the pieced triangles slightly off.

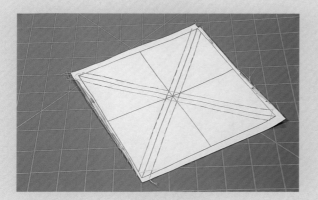

2. Decrease the stitch length on your machine to 1.5. Tearing the paper away once the block is pieced can alter the stitch if it is not decreased. Paper piece the triangles using the 6-1/2" squares of fabrics. Pair up a solid with a print, right sides together, place the triangle grid paper over the fabrics and sew on the dotted lines of the grid.

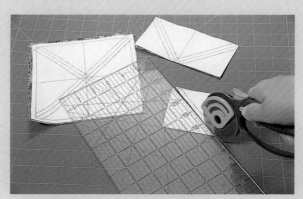

3. Rotary cut on the solid lines of the grid.

4. Tear the paper away and press the seam towards the darker fabric. You will have 56 half square triangles.

5. Place the squares around the 12-1/2" x 18-1/2" rectangle. Arrange their placement until you have a pleasing design.

6. Sew two strips of six squares together for top and bottom.

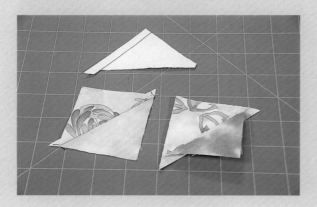

7. Sew these strips to the top and bottom of the 12-1/2" x 18-1/2" rectangle.

8. Sew two strips of eleven squares together and sew them to the sides of the center rectangle.

quiltedpetal

9. Sew the two 3-1/2″ x 16-1/2″ outer borders to the top and bottom of the quilt.

10. Sew the two 3-1/2″ x 28-1/2″ outer borders to each side of the quilt.

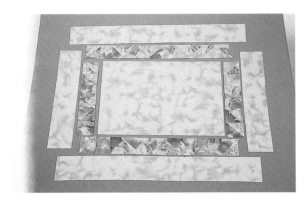

11. Layer the top with the batting and the backing. Since you have one yard of the backing fabric, you can play with the placement and get the flowers of the backing fabric in the desired location on your quilt. Once you have your backing placement, trim the back to 26″ x 32″.

12. Pin baste the quilt with the large floral fabric on the top. Your actual quilt top will play as the quilt back when you are pinning. The pin heads will be on the large floral (or backing) fabric.

13. Set your machine up for free motion quilting with your feed dogs down and the darning foot on. Put a fun decorative thread in the bobbin, as it will be the thread that will appear on the quilt top. I used red in the bobbin when quilting the petals of flowers and a green in the bobbin while quilting leaves of the flowers. I also matched thread colors in the needle and in the bobbin when quilting this project.

14. Free motion quilt around each leaf and petal, paying attention to your bobbin tension. Try to connect the motifs you are quilting even if the fabric design does not connect them. Each time you start and stop you need to make a few stitches in place, which creates a small knot on the top of the quilt. Try to limit these numbers of starts and stops. Machine quilt the entire quilt.

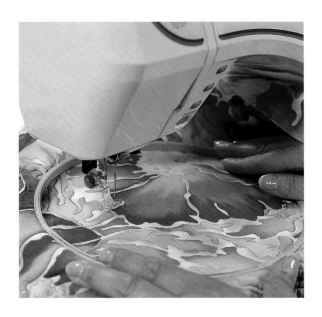

15. Turn the quilt over, and using the crayons, shade the outside edges of each petal and leaf. Use reds for the flowers and greens for the leaves. Use a light touch and a flat side of the crayon. Shade the entire quilt top as desired.

16. Cover the quilt top with a paper towel. With a cotton setting, iron over the paper towel. This will heat-set the crayons. Some of the wax will come through to the paper towel. Ironing or heat-setting the crayon will lighten the coloring slightly. You can add more color if you choose, and heat-set again.

17. Hand sew beads for embellishment. Cover the thread starts and stops with the beads.

Finishing Options

• This quilt was designed to fit in a 22" x 28" frame. It looks great behind glass!

• Binding is another finishing option. If you choose to bind the quilt, use 1/4" binding.

Glowbug

Finished Size:
12" wide x 11" from nose to tail.
Patterns pages 137-138

- 1/4 yard of dark background fabric

- 7 different brightly colored scraps of fabric for the bug body parts

- 8" square of fabric for the wings. Note: the upper wings can be a different fabric from the lower wings, in that case, you will need 8" squares of two different wing fabrics.

- Scraps for eyes and neck

- YLI Fine Metallic thread for lace wings

- Cotton thread for bobbin

- 1/3 yard of tulle netting

- 1/3 yard of Sulky Heat Away Stabilizer

- 8" wooden machine embroidery hoop

- 90/14 machine embroidery needles

- Photocopy of the bug paper-piecing pattern (Be sure the photocopy of your pattern is exactly like the original pattern and the machine has not distorted it.)

Mom came to visit one week in January of 2001. Whenever she comes to visit, we always have fun! We go out to lunch, get our nails done, and sometimes sew. This time we just sewed.

I had this bug drawn out for a new design for this book. I hadn't actually pieced it together yet, and thought it would be a great project for the two of us to do together. We had three days together, and we could get a good start on it.

She got busy paper piecing the bugs and making lace for the wings while I worked on the inside of the quilt. I played with sashings and did some embellishing with a hand-dyed rick rack. Before we knew it, the quilt was basically done!

This quilt just kind of flew together on its own. I think mom was surprised how quickly it all happened. She wasn't even done making the bugs, and I was writing the instructions for it.

The quilt represents where I am today: happy, glowing and flying free. I wonder how my life could get any better than it is at this very moment. I truly believe that our attitude has a direct affect on our lives. I tried to focus my energy into something productive, and create something positive from the "cards" that I was dealt. Our custody battle was finally over and I came out a stronger person in the end, and am so thankful to be finally set free!

The following are instructions and supplies for completing one Glow Bug block. The bug can have lace wings or just fabric wings. The lace making technique can be used in many other quilting projects.

Glowbug

Basic Paper Piecing Instructions

1. Set your machine stitch length to a 1.5.

2. Cut a piece of fabric large enough to cover the area #1 with at least a 1/4" seam allowance.

3. Place wrong side of fabric #1 over space #1 on the unprinted side of the pattern.

4. Place fabric #2 right sides together with fabric #1, on the unprinted side of the pattern, being sure the fabric is 1/4" over the desired seam line.

5. Stitch on the line between the numbered area being added and the one previously covered.

6. Trim the seam to 1/4", without cutting the paper.

7. Press the added fabric open, being sure it completely covers the numbered area.

8. Continue with all numbered fabrics until all patterns are complete.

9. Trim final piece 1/4" beyond the stitching line completely around the pattern. Tear paper away if desired.

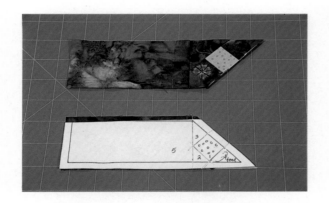

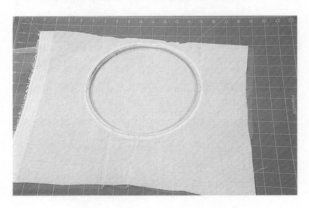

Basic Bug Instructions

1. Paper piece all sections of the bug EXCLUDING THE WINGS according to the Basic Paper Piecing Instructions.

2. Be sure to trim the sections 1/4" beyond the outer stitching lines of the patterns.

3. Sew the two eye sections together along the diagonal line. Refer to the line drawing of the pattern if needed.

4. Sew the body sections together being sure the neck is at the top of the strip section. Section one will be sewn to section two then to section three.

Making Lace for Wings

1. Cut a 10"x 18" piece of tulle and stabilizer.

2. Layer the tulle netting over the stabilizer and secure it in the machine embroidery hoop with the screw closure on the bottom of the fabric. The hoop should be flush with the sewing machine table. Tighten the tulle and stabilizer taking care not to tear them.

3. Set your machine up for free motion sewing by lowering the feed dogs, adding darning foot and slightly loosening your top tension. Thread the needle of the machine with the fine metallic thread and matching cotton in the bobbin.

Glowbug

4. Begin filling up the hoop with thread by moving the hoop in round circular motions. Keep in mind that the faster you go with your foot, the more control you will have. Be careful not to overdo the thread, you want some "air" to show through. Stitch your circles over one another to secure the lace. Make enough lace to do all four sections of the wings plus 4". The lace will shrink slightly once it is ironed. Move the hoop as needed to get the lace section you need completed.

NOTE: If you have trouble with your machine when making the lace with the metallic threaded through the needle, try putting the metallic thread in the bobbin and the cotton thread through the needle.

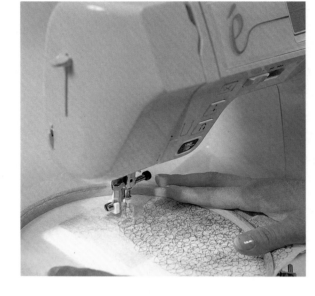

5. Using a hot dry iron, burn off the stabilizer. Be careful not to burn the netting. Move the iron as you heat up the stabilizer. It will begin to turn brown to black. You can iron both sides of the lace.

6. Hold the lace over a garbage can and crinkle the lace between your hands to remove the stabilizer. Now you will have lace, made from thread, secured by tulle netting.

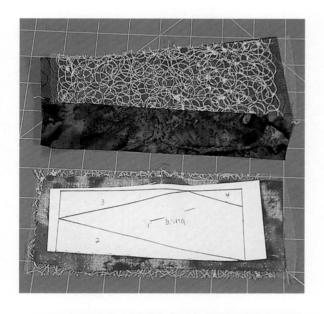

Paper Piecing the Lace Wing Sections

1. Place the fabric for the wing over space #1 on the unprinted side of the pattern with the right side out. Layer a piece of lace over the wing fabric, being sure the lace and fabric are both at least 1/4" larger than the pattern around all four sides.

2. Place fabric #2 right sides together over the wing fabric and lace, with at least 1/4" seam allowance over the desired seam line. Stitch on the line. Trim seam to 1/4" and press.

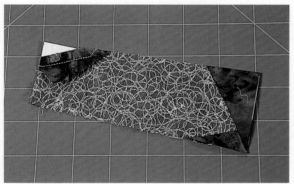

3. Place fabric #3 right sides together over the wing fabric and lace, with at least 1/4" seam allowance over the desired seam line. Stitch on the line. Trim seam to 1/4" and press. Continue in the same manner with fabric #4.

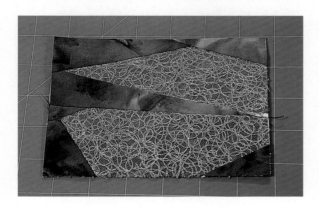

4. Trim the lace wing 1/4" beyond the stitching line.

5. Continue making the other three sections of the wings in this manner.

6. Sew the top and bottom wing section together.

Glowbug

Completing the Glow Bug Block

1. Sew the top and bottom wing sections together on both sides of the bug. Press the seam.

2. Make a template from the square diagram, adding 1/4" seam allowance on page 137.

3. Sew the background square to the bottom of the wing sections on both sides of the bug. Press the seam.

4. Sew each side of the wings to the body right sides together. Press the seam towards the wing. Sew rectangles to the sides of the head.

5. Sew the head to the wing and body section right sides together. Press the seam towards the head.

Options

The wings of the Glow Bug can be made with fabric and lace combination, or they can be just fabric. The top and bottom wing on each side of the bug can also be changed. My mom accidentally pieced the bug's wings wrong, the lower wing on the pattern is actually pieced as the upper wing on my quilt. We figured this out after most of the bugs were made! I told her it was not a mistake, and they can actually be done however it pleases you! This made her feel better.

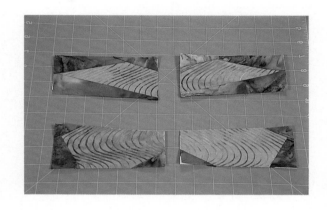

Instructions for Center Blocks
(Yields four blocks)

1. Stack 4 different fabrics on top of each other and cut them 14" x 14".

2. With a ruler and rotary cutter, cut an "X" through the center of the stack.

3. Now rearrange the order of the fabrics so that all four sections of the block are different.

4. Sew the 4 sections together.

5. Trim to the finished size of the glow bug block, 12" x 11".

skinnyhearts

Finished size: 50.5" wide by 58.5" long

supplies

- 1/4 yards of 10-12 different light background fabrics (look at both sides of the fabric, as you will be using the backs too!)

- Fat 1/8's of 10 to 20 different dark pink to red fabrics for the hearts

- 1/4 yard of narrow dark border

- 1 yard of fabric for outer border

- 1/6 yard of fabric for corner squares, or one extra fat quarter.

*S*kinny Hearts represents the hearts that have come my way. Thin, fragile, easily broken, empty inside, and not quite put together right.

I had fun making this quilt, and it reaffirms to me not just to "settle". I will wait for a strong, complete, full and well-rounded heart.

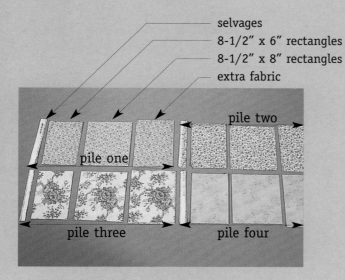

selvages
8-1/2" x 6" rectangles
8-1/2" x 8" rectangles
extra fabric

pile one
pile two
pile three
pile four

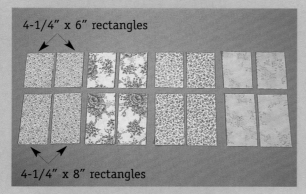

4-1/4" x 6" rectangles

4-1/4" x 8" rectangles

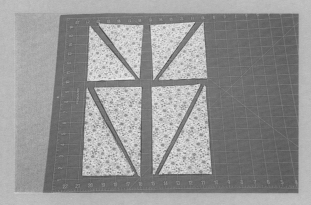

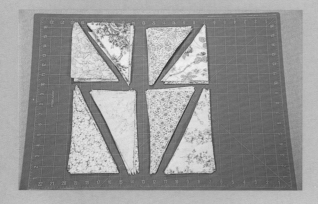

1. Fold the background fabrics as you bought them with wrong sides together and selvages even.

2. Evenly divide all of the background fabrics (uncut) into 4 different piles for ease in rotary cutting. Trim off selvages. Cut 8-1/2" x 6" rectangle and 8-1/2" x 8" rectangle from each set. You will have two rectangle sets of each fabric in each of the two sizes. Leave them stacked in the piles that you have cut.

3. Cut the 8-1/2" x 6" rectangles in half into 4-1/4" x 6" sets.

4. Cut the 8-1/2" x 8" rectangles in half into 4-1/4" x 8" sets. Leave them stacked as you have them-in piles. Save the extra background fabric for sashings.

5. Now cut these sets in half from corner to corner. Be sure you cut them in the right direction as shown in photo.

6. Now stack all your same cuts in the same pile so it looks like this: mix up the order so that you have 8 different backgrounds in each layer, keep in mind that you will be using the back side of the fabric also. Don't put it in another pile. Leave it where it is, and you will actually have about 20 different fabrics now

skinny**hearts**

7. Now cut the red fabrics into 1" strips. Put them all in a pile and mix them up! Sew them randomly in the center of each triangle section using a scant 1/4" seam, like this:

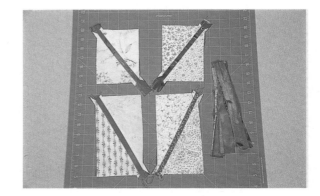

8. Randomly choose red strips and sew them to the side of each of the 4-1/4" x 6" triangle sets so it looks like this.

9. Trim the 4-1/4" x 6" blocks to 4" x 5-1/2" but do NOT trim from the red side!

10. Trim the 4-1/4" x 8" blocks to 4" x 7-1/2".

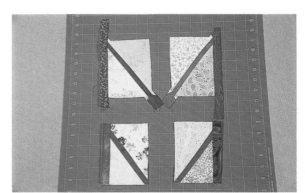

11. Sew the two top sections of the heart together.

12. Sew the two bottom sections of the heart together.

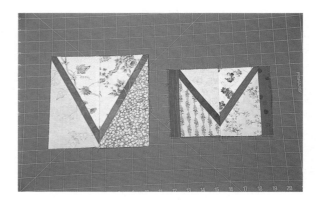

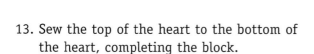

13. Sew the top of the heart to the bottom of the heart, completing the block.

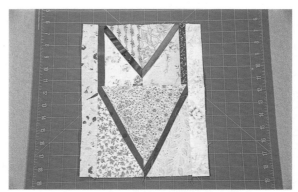

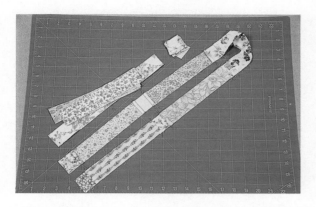

Sashing

14. Cut the remaining background pieces into 1-1/2" strips. Then cut them into 25 (1-1/2" x 7-1/2") pieces and 24 (1-1/2" x 12-1/2") pieces. Make sure all the backgrounds are represented.

15. Cut 30 (1-1/2") squares from the backgrounds.

16. Sew the 7-1/2" sashing strips and corner squares together like this.

17. Sew the 12-1/2" sashing strips to the sides of the heart blocks.

18. Sew the sashed hearts to the rows of sashing.

19. Cut the skinny border 1" and sew it to the quilt.

20. Cut the outer border to 5" and sew it to the quilt, piecing in the 5" corner square blocks. Refer to the quilt photo as needed.

21. Quilt as desired. Refer to Drawing with Machine Needle chapter for quilting ideas.

22. Bind the quilt with 1/4" binding.

Somewhat Off Center. Photo by Tilton

Finishing Touches:
Binding Your Quilts for a Professional Look

The success of any quilt, no matter how beautiful, is influenced by how skillfully the edges are finished. There are many ways that the edges of a quilt can be finished. The choice may depend on the quilt and the wishes of the artist.

The most common finishes are bindings. Applied bindings use additional fabric for the binding. Edge turned bindings are made by folding the fabric from the backing over to the top of the quilt. Other less common finishes include piping, or corded edges, prairie points, lace, ruffles and fringe. These bindings are all very interesting and fun on the right quilt, but most of my quilts have the regular applied binding.

Grain

Some people prefer bias binding, but I do not like to use it. I find that it is harder to handle and to apply and feel that it has a tendency to pull the quilt out of shape. It also takes more fabric. You must use bias bindings on curves. Cross-grain bindings are cut with the length of the strips at right angles to the selvages. I prefer cross-grain bindings because it has just a small amount of stretch if the edges of the quilt are rippled. You can also run basting stitches around the quilt, if the edges are rippled, and pull the basting thread slightly to ease in the ripple.

Quilters who prefer bias bindings believe that it wears better than straight-grain bindings because the fibers in the fabric are not aligned with the edge of the quilt. A straight grain binding cut exactly on grain will have one fiber running along the edge, and this thread would get the bulk of the wear and stress.

While this would be true of bindings cut on the lengthwise grain, which is very straight and strong, it is rarely true with bindings cut across the fabric on the cross grain. Most crosswise threads in today's fabrics do not run perfectly straight across from selvage to selvage, so there would not be one single fiber running exactly along the edge of the binding. It would wear almost as well as bias.[1]

[1] *The Quilters Ultimate Visual Guide*, Ellen Paul editor, Rodale Press, Emmaus, Pennsylvania, 1997, p.43- 44

finishing touches

Quality Bindings...What are Judges Looking For?

1. **Is the binding filled with batting?**
The binding should be completely filled with the quilt sandwich. There should be no flat part on the fold edge of the binding that is not filled with batting.

2. **Is the binding width appropriate to the quilt?**
This is somewhat of an individual, and personal preference. If there is piecing that extends to the outer edge of the quilt, 1/4" binding is preferred so that the piecing is not covered too much. If there is no piecing on the outer edge of the quilt, I prefer 1/4" to 1/2" binding.

3. **Are the corners nicely mitered on top and back?**
The corners of the binding should have nice miters on the front as well as the back of the quilt.

4. **Are the edges of the binding on the back even with the edges of the binding on the front?**
The front fold edge of the binding should line up with the back fold edge of the binding. Stitch the back down by hand so that the edge of the binding is just slightly over the machine stitching used to apply the binding.

5. **Is the binding sewn down with invisible hand stitches?**
Quality bindings are sewn down by hand on the back of the quilt so that the stitches do not show.

6. **Are the binding strips mitered?**
The binding strips should be mitered at 45 degrees to ease in bulk when the binding is turned around the edge of the quilt.

7. **Is the start/stop of the binding mitered?**
The beginning and ending, or where it meets, should be mitered also.

Preparing the quilt

Be sure the quilt lies flat and the corners and edges are accurate and square. The corners should be 90 degrees, if they are not, trim them with a square ruler. The more care that is taken at this point, the better the edges will finish.

If the edges of your quilt are slightly rippled, baste around the quilt with stitches about 1/2" long. Then lay the edge on a flat surface and gently gather it until it lies flat. Stay stitch by hand or machine to hold it in place, then sew the binding on.

Making a Show Regulation Rod Pocket

I like to make my pockets out of the same fabric as the backing fabric so they are less noticeable. This step has to be done before the binding is sewn on.

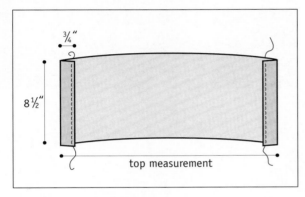

3/4"

8½"

top measurement

1. Measure the top of your quilt where pocket is to go. Your rod pocket will need to be cut that top measurement by 8-1/2" wide.

2. Press under each short end of the rod pocket 3/4" and stitch.

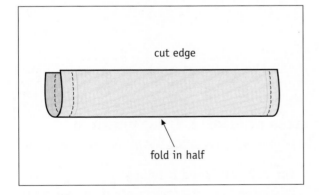

cut edge

fold in half

3. Fold the rod pocket in half, with wrong sides together, the entire length and press.

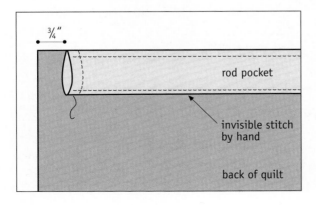

3/4"

rod pocket

invisible stitch by hand

back of quilt

4. Pin it to the top edge of the back of the quilt after the quilt has been squared. The raw edges of the rod pocket and the quilt must be even, and the rod pocket should be about 3/4" in from both edges.

5. Baste the rod pocket using a scant 1/4" seam allowance. Then you can proceed with sewing the binding onto the quilt. The binding should be sewn on the back side of the quilt. Hand stitch the fold of the rod pocket down with an invisible stitch after hand stitching the binding down.

Binding Your Quilts for a Professional Look

Applied Binding

With single fold binding it is much easier to achieve good mitered corners. They can be neatly sewn.

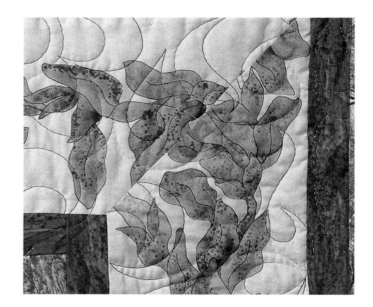

Double fold binding is cut at 2.5 inches, for 1/4" finished binding. It is pressed in half first and the raw edges of the binding are placed even with the quilt top and then sewn 1/4". Once it is turned over the edge of the quilt, the fold of the binding is stitched down, thus leaving no room to adjust the binding to get it to come exactly even with the stitching line since it is double thickness. Some people believe it wears better than single fold binding.

Cutting the Binding Strips

1. Fold the binding fabric selvage to selvage.
   Make sure the fabric is folded straight.

2. Rotary cut a straight edge on the fabric, and
   then proceed to rotary cut the binding strips.

Formula for cutting strips for different sizes of SINGLE FOLD bindings

Cut one extra strip more than the measurement of the perimeter of the quilt, to guarantee enough strips.

For 1/4" finished binding
(using a 1/4" presser foot)
1/4" seam + 1/4" fold over + 1/4" fudge factor +
1/4" fold over + 1/4" pressed edge = 1-1/4"
Cut strips 1-1/4"

For 1/2" finished binding
(mark the 1/2" seam allowance on machine plate)
1/2" seam + 1/2" fold over + 1/4" fudge
factor + 1/2" fold over + 1/4" pressed edge = 2"
Cut strips 2"

General formula for your own widths

(desired width) seam **+** (desired width) fold over **+**
1/4" fudge factor **+** (desired width) fold over **+** 1/4"
pressed edge **=** strip width to cut

Sewing Together and Pressing the Binding Strips

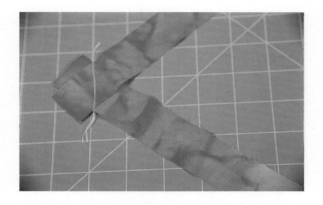

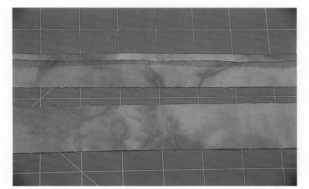

1. It is important to piece the binding strips together at a 45-degree angle. Piecing them at a 45-degree angle decreases the bulk from the seam as the binding is folded over the edge of the quilt. Press the seam open to reduce bulk.

2. Press one edge of the entire length of the binding under 1/4".

Sewing Binding Strips to the Quilt:

1. Lay the binding strip out roughly on the quilt to find a starting point. You want to be sure that areas where you joined the strips do not fall on the corners. If they end up at the corners, it will be additional bulk and affect the miter at the corner.

2. Begin by folding the edge of the binding to form a triangle. Sew the binding onto the right side of the quilt, using the seam allowance for the size of binding you have chosen for your quilt. If you are sewing 1/2" binding, you need a 1/2" seam allowance. If you are making 1/4" binding, you need a 1/4" seam allowance.

Finishing Touches:
Binding Your Quilts for a Professional Look

Folding the Mitered Corners

1. Stop sewing 1/4" from the edge of the corner of the quilt for 1/4" binding and backstitch. For 1/2" binding, stop sewing 1/2" from the edge of the quilt and backstitch. Fold the binding back onto itself at a 45 degree angle

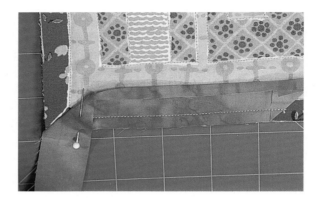

2. Fold the binding again keeping the 45 degree angle while folding the binding back on itself with the edge of the binding even with the edge of the quilt. Begin sewing again, from the edge of the quilt. It is not necessary to back stitch here.

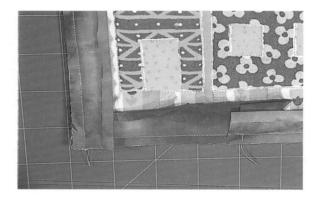

Finishing the Binding

I use an invisible hand stitch to secure my binding on the back. It is sort of a sideways 's' stitch.

1. Hide your single knotted thread in the binding, then go into the fold of the binding, grab the quilt and batting, taking care not to go through the complete quilt and through the back, run the needle about an 1/8" through the batting then come back up to the top of the edge of the binding.

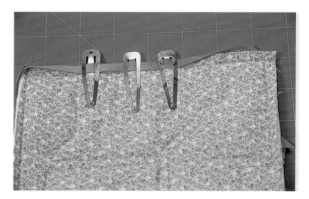

2. Insert the needle back into the hole you just came up and continue the same stitch.

3. Hide your knots when you start stitching the binding in the layers of the quilt. When you run out of thread, make as small a knot as possible on the very edge of the binding. Then run the thread through the quilt to hide the tail, bring it up to the back of the quilt and cut the thread off.

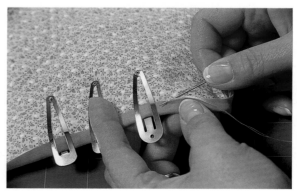

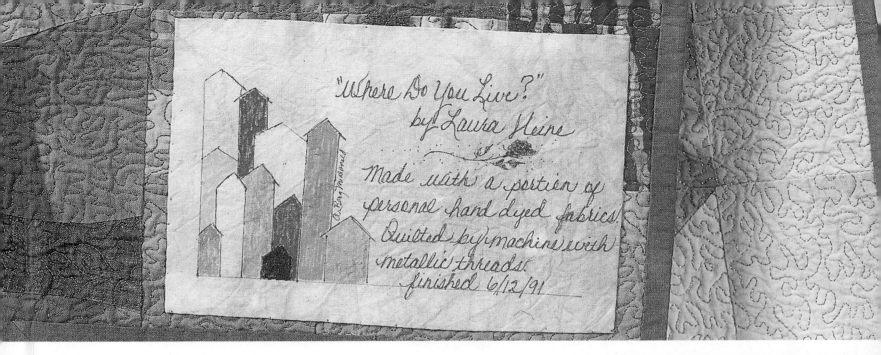

Quilt Labels

The quilt label is very important because it provides information about your quilt for history. It is the best way to provide accurate information to be passed from generation to generation, and it stays with the quilt. It also provides a finishing and somewhat personal touch to the quilt.

Labels can be very simple, or very elegant. They can be unused blocks from the front of the quilt. There are also preprinted labels available today to make your life easy!

It is important to document certain information on the label:

- The name of the quilt.
- The name of the quiltmaker.
- The year the quilt was completed.
- Where the quilt was completed.
- The name of the recipient of the quilt.
- An address and phone number in case the quilt is lost.
- Any personal messages.

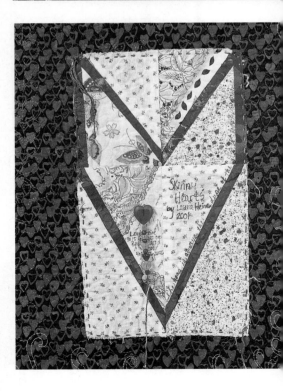

- Permanent fabric pen such as a Pigma or Identipen

- 100% cotton fabric for the label

- Freezer paper for stabilization

Procedure

1. Decide what you want to put on the label. Make a rough draft on paper first.

2. Iron the wrong side of the fabric for the label to the shiny side of freezer paper. This will stabilize the fabric for ease in writing.

3. Using the fabric pens, write the information on the label, refer to the rough draft as needed.

4. Add small beads, buttons or other embellishments if desired.

5. Color can be added with crayons. Refer to the Quilted Petal chapter for coloring techniques.

6. Remove the freezer paper from the back of the label.

7. Press under 1/4" seam allowance around all edges of the label.

8. Appliqué the label to the lower right corner of the back of the quilt.

The label of your quilt will make it different and unique. Take pride in your workmanship and document the important information on your labels!

Jane's Quilt

enlarge 200%

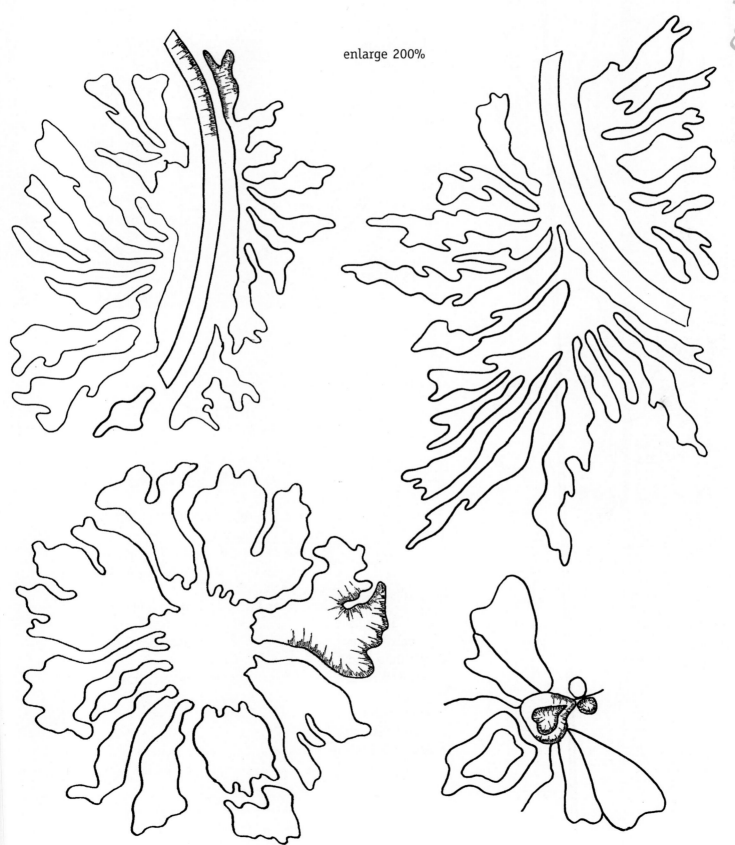

Floret
Quilted Petal
Jane's Quilt

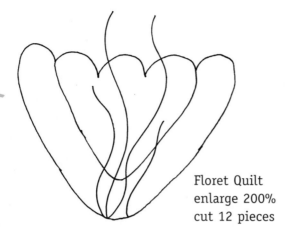

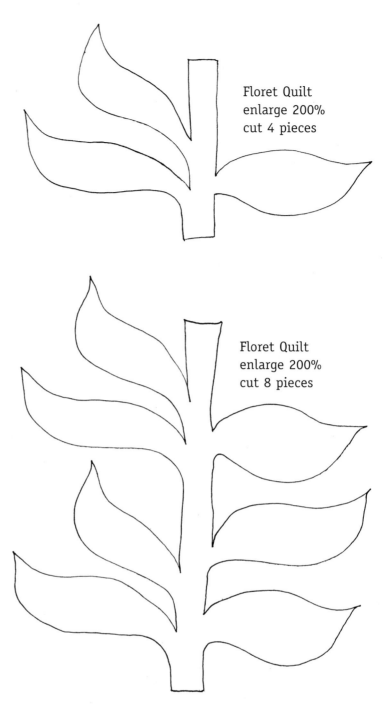

Floret Quilt
enlarge 200%
cut 4 pieces

Floret Quilt
enlarge 200%
cut 12 pieces

Floret Quilt
enlarge 200%
cut 8 pieces

Floret Quilt
enlarge 200%
cut 5 pieces

Quilted Petal
Placement
guide

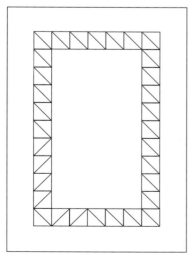

Triangle
pattern for
Jane's Quilt and
Quilted Petal

enlarge 200%
to finish at
5-3/4" x 5-3/4"

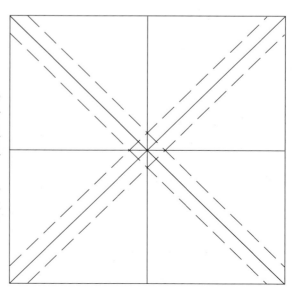

Glow Bug

Glow Bug pattern pieces
enlarge 200%

Body Parts

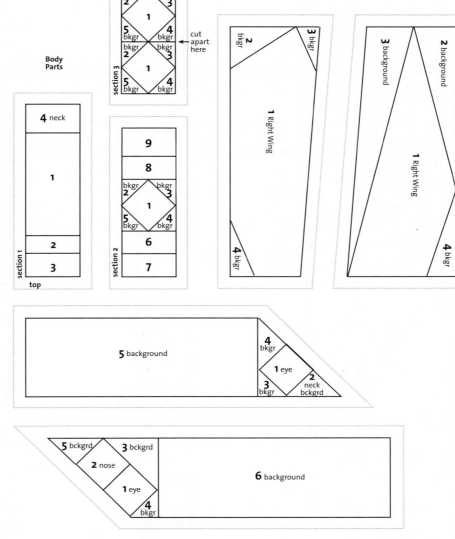

section 3

bkgr 2	bkgr 3
1	
5 bkgr	4 bkgr
bkgr 2	bkgr 3
1	
5 bkgr	4 bkgr

← cut apart here

section 1

| 4 neck |
| 1 |
| 2 |
| 3 |

top

section 2

| 9 |
| 8 |
bkgr 2	bkgr 3
1	
5 bkgr	4 bkgr
6
7

2 bkgr — 1 Right Wing — 3 bkgr — 4 bkgr

3 background — 2 background — 1 Right Wing — 4 bkgr

5 background — 4 bkgr — 1 eye — 2 neck bckgrd — 3 bkgr

5 bckgrd — 3 bckgrd — 2 nose — 1 eye — 6 background — 4 bkgr

background template

3 background — 2 background — 1 Left Wing — 4 bkgr

3 bkgr — 2 bkgr — 1 Left Wing — 4 bkgr

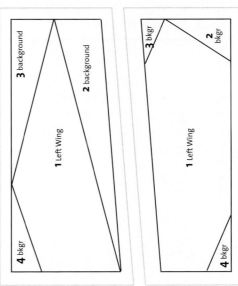

Glow Bug

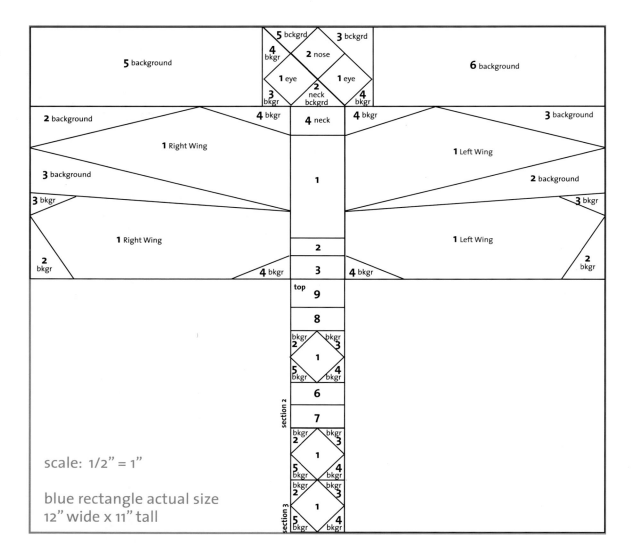

scale: 1/2" = 1"

blue rectangle actual size
12" wide x 11" tall

Glow Bug template
enlarge 200%

Finished size:
12"wide x 11" nose to tail

resources

A&E AMERICAN & EFIRD INC.
400 East Central Ave
Mt. Holly, NC 28120
800-847-3235
www.amefird.com

AMERICAN QUILTERS SOCIETY
Box 3290
Paducah, KY 42002
502-898-7903

BABYLOCK
1760 Gilsinn Lane
Fenton, MO 63026
800-428-8663
www.babylock.com

BALI FABRICS
554 Third St. West
Sonoma, CA 95476
800-783-4612
www.balifab.com

BERNINA
3500 Thayer Court
Aurora, IL 60504
800-877-0477
www.bernina.com

DRAGON THREADS
410 Canyon Drive North
Columbus, OH 43214
614-267-2914
FAX 614-267-2945
www.dragonthreads.com
Laura's notecards, other sewing
books and supplies.

CINDY EDGERTON
208 Tabb Lakes Drive
Yorktown, VA 23692
757-867-7711
www.averyspecialcollection.com
"A Very Special Collection "
BIG BLOCK patterns

ELNA
1760 Gilsinn Lane
Fenton, MO 63026
800-428-8663
www.elnausa.com

FIBERWORKS
1310 24th Street West
Billings, MT 59102
406-656-6663
fax 406-656-3363
email: laurah@fiberworks-
heine.com
All Laura's fabrics, patterns,
notecards and supplies.

FISKARS
7811 West Stewart Avenue
Wausau, WI 54402
800-950-0203

HOFFMAN FABRICS
25792 Obrero Drive
Mission Viejo, CA 92691-3140
800-547-0100
www.hoffmanfabrics.com

HUSQVARNA VIKING
31000 Viking Pkwy.
Westlake, OH 44145
www.husqvarnaviking.com

**INTERNATIONAL QUILT
FESTIVAL**
7660 Wood Way #550
Houston, TX 77063
713-781-6864
www.quilts.com

KINGS ROAD IMPORTS
548 South Los Angeles Street
Los Angeles, CA 90013
800-433-1546
www.kingsrd.com

**DIONE ROBERTS,
D&J's GLASSWORKS**
502 Grand Avenue
Billings, MT 59101
406-259-4469
www.stainedglassretailers.com
/DJhome

RODALE PRESS
33 East Minor Street
Emmaus, PA 18098
www.rodale.com

SULKY
3113 Broadpoint Drive
Harbor Heights, FL 33983
800-874-4115
www.sulky.com

YLI
161 West Main Street
Rock Hill, SC 29730
800-296-8139
www.ylicorp.com

THE WARM COMPANY
954 East Union St.
Seattle, WA 98122
800-234-WARM
Steam-A-Seam 2

bibliography

Amsden, Deirdre, *Colorwash Quilts*; 1994, That Patchwork Place

Hartman, Dr. Taylor, *Color Code*; 1987, Simon & Schuster

Heine, Laura, *Appliqué Made Easy*; 1998, Rodale Inc., opening page

Heine, Laura, *Choosing Quilting Designs*; 2001, Rodale Inc. pp.18, 64-71, 122-3

Heine, Laura, *Creative Embellishments*; 2001, Rodale Inc.

Heine, Laura, *Fast and Fun Machine Quilting*; 1999, Rodale Inc. pp. 20-25 and cover

Heine, Laura, *Favorite Techniques From the Experts*; 2000, Rodale Inc. pp. 96-101 and back cover

Margaret, Pat Maixner and Slusser, Donna, *Watercolor Impressions*; 1995, That Patchwork Place, pp. 68-9

Paul, Ellen, *The Quilter's Ultimate Visual Guide*; 1997, Rodale Inc., pp. 43- 44

Piecemakers, Colorsplash, Trip Around the World; 1995, Piecemakers

Stoddard, Alexandra, *Alexandra Stoddard's Book of Color*; 1998, Doubleday Publishing

Wilder, Donna, *A Field of Flower Quilts*; 1994, American School of Needlework

Wolfrom, Joen, *Patchwork Persuasion*; 1997, C&T Publishing, page 129

Wolfrom, Joen, *The Visual Dance*; 1995, C&T Publishing, page 141

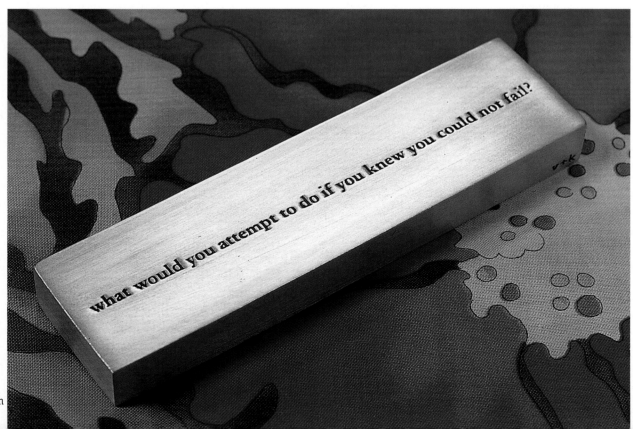

Country Hearts and Homes
1st Place, Western Heritage Center,
Billings, MT 1986

Star of Hearts
Honorable Mention, Lamplighter Quilt Show,
Billings, MT 1987

Fancy Fans
2nd Place, Western Heritage Center,
Billings, MT 1987

Pinwheel Star
1st Place, Women in Art, Billings, MT 1990
3rd Place, State Fair, Great Falls, MT 1990

English Influence
2nd Place, Western Heritage Center,
Billings, MT 1990
1st Place, Billings Art Association,
Billings, MT 1991

Light From Within
3rd Place, Women in Art, Billings, MT 1991
Best Use of Color, Western Heritage Center,
Billings, MT 1991
1st Place, Montana State Fair, Billings, MT 1993

My View of the World
3rd Place, Miles City Quilt Show,
Miles City, MT 1991
3rd Place, American Quilter's Society,
Paducah, KY 1992
1st Place, Fabric of Our Cultures,
Victoria, TX 1993

Where Do You Live?
1st Place and Judges' Choice, Montana State Fair,
Billings, MT 1991
1st Place, Women in Art, Billings, MT 1992

Best of Both Worlds
1st Place, Western Heritage Center,
Billings, MT 1992
Best Use of Color, Western Heritage Center,
Billings, MT 1992
Award of Excellence, International Quilt Assoc,
Houston, TX 1992
Discovery Award, Arts Chateau, Butte, MT 1993
Best Entry from Montana Award, Arts Chateau,
Butte, MT 1993

How Does Your Garden Grow?
1st Place, Labor of Love Contest,
Billings, MT 1992
Viewers' Choice Overall, International Quilt
Association, Houston, TX 1992

I Valued My Plaids
Frances Barnhardt Memorial Award,
Western Heritage Center, Billings, MT 1993

A Rose is a Rose is a Rose
People's Choice, Great American Quilt Festival,
Logan, UT 1993

Opposing Forces
Merchants' Choice Award-Flight of Imagination,
Euphrata, PA 1993

One Fish, Two Fish, Red Fish, Blue Fish
Honorable Mention, International Quilt Assoc,
Houston TX 1994
Bernina Purchase Award, American Quilter's
Society, Paducah, KY 1994

Kaleidoscope Krazy
Best of Show and 1st Place Art Quilt, Western
Heritage Center, Billings, MT 1994
Award of Excellence, International Quilt Festival,
Houston, TX 1994
2nd Place, Fabric of Our Cultures,
Victoria, TX 1996

Big Fish; Small Pond
Award of Excellence, International
Quilt Festival, Houston, TX 1995
1st Place Art Quilt and Best Use of Color,
Western Heritage Center, Billings, MT 1996
Best of Show, Quilting in the Tetons,
Jackson, WY 1996
1st Masters Division, Fabric of Our Cultures,
Victoria, TX 1997

Jerry's Star
3rd Place Group Quilt, Western Heritage Center,
Billings, MT 1996

Leftovers
3rd Place, International Quilt Festival,
Houston, TX 1997

We Three
3rd Place, Western Heritage Center,
Billings, MT 1998

Somewhat Off Center
2nd Place, Pacific International Quilt Association,
Seattle, WA 1996

Turning Over a New Leaf
Judges' Choice, International Quilt Festival,
Houston, TX 1998

Divine Inspiration
3rd Choice, International Quilt Festival,
Houston, TX 1999

publications

American Quilter, Fall 1992, Vol. VIII, No. 3

Lady's Circle Patchwork Quilts, January 1993

Quilter's Newsletter Magazine, March 1992, No. 250

Lady's Circle Patchwork Quilts, July 1993

Editor's Choice From Patchwork Quilts' Quilt Craft,
    1993, No. 1

American Quilter, Spring 1994, Vol. X, No. 1

American Quilter's Society, Wall Calendar, 1995

American Quilter, Fall 1994, Vol X, No. 3

Quilter's Newsletter Magazine, April 1995, No. 271

That Patchwork Place, Fall Catalog, 1995

Quilts, A World of Beauty, AIQA Special Issue, 1993

Quilts, A World of Beauty, AIQA Fall 1995 (cover)

The Visual Dance, by Joen Wolfrom

Watercolor Impressions,
    by Pat Maixner Magaret and Donna Slusser

YLI Decorative Threads Brochure, 1996 (cover)

American Quilter's Society, Postcards, 1996

Creative Needle, Holiday Sale Magazine,
September/October1996

Quilter's Newsletter Magazine,
    December 1996, No. 288

Montana Magazine,
    November/December 1996, No. 140

Buyer's Guide, International Quilt Market,
    Fall 1996

Sew Beautiful, Holiday Issue, 1996

Quilts, A World of Beauty, Fall 1996

Buyer's Guide, International Quilt Market,
    Spring 1997

Patchwork Persuasion, by Joen Wolfrom

Sew Beautiful, Spring 1997

Creative Needle, May/June 1997

Sew Beautiful, Fall 1997

Fast and Fun Machine Quilting, Rodale Press, 1999

Appliqué Made Easy, Rodale Press

Saint Vincent Hospital Calendar, 1999

Quilter's Newsletter Magazine,
    January 1999, No. 309

Quilter's Newsletter Magazine,
    March 1999, No. 310

Quilter's Newsletter Magazine,
    April 1999, No. 311 (back cover)

Quilter's Newsletter Magazine,
    June 1999, No. 313 (back cover)

The Creative Needle, 1999, Vol. VIX, No. 1

CAN, August 1999, pg. 87

Buyer's Guide, International Quilt Market,
    Fall 2000 (inside back cover)

Favorite Techniques From the Experts,
    Rodale Press, 2000

Choosing Quilting Designs, Rodale Press, 2001

Creative Embellishments, Rodale Press, 2001

The Creative Needle, Vol. X, No. 4,
    Fall 2000, pg. 43

Quilter's Newsletter Magazine,
    April 2000, No. 321, pg. 81

Quilter's Newsletter Magazine,
    July/August 2000, No. 324 (back cover)

Quilter's Newsletter Magazine,
    October 2000, No. 326 (back cover)

Quilter's Newsletter Magazine,
    December 2000, No. 328, pg. 38-40 & back cover

MAQS Quilts: The Founders' Collection,
    published by the Museum of the American
    Quilters' Society, Paducah, KY, 2001

index

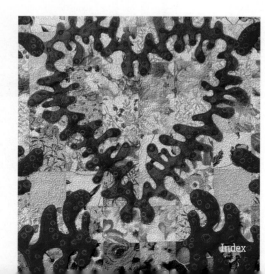

Together...Jenna, Laura & Brandon Heine, 2001, 37" x 35"   *photo by Daniel Tilton*

Inspirational stories on how quilting helped Laura overcome her adversity.

From Thought to Cloth . . . how Laura designs her quilt fabric line.

Award-winning quilting techniques and secrets to Color Fusion.

5 Beautiful original quilt designs.

Photography by Kelvin

Laura is an award winning quilt artist who wins top prizes for her intricate free-motion thread work that fuses her colors, fabrics and design into one amazing quilt! Trained as a nurse, she started out just wanting to make one quilt for her first baby. Now, 15 years later, she is one of the top quilters in the world, a national educator, fabric designer, author, thread company consultant, pattern designer and quilt shop owner. Read about her inspirational journey to discover the talent that was hidden inside her and how she developed it into her sensational style.

Dragon Threads